The Americans in Action, 1918

The Americans in Action, 1918

The First Battles: Cantigny, Château Thierry
& the Second Battle of the Marne

Jennings C. Wise

With Additional Illustrations by
Jean Berne-Bellecour
and
An Address by
Otto H. Kahn

LEONAUR

The Americans in Action, 1918
The First Battles: Cantigny, Château Thierry & the Second Battle of the Marne
by Jennings C. Wise
With Additional Illustrations by Jean Berne-Bellecour
and an Address by Otto H. Kahn

First published under the title
The Turn of the Tide

Leonaur is an imprint of Oakpast Ltd

Copyright in this form © 2014 Oakpast Ltd

ISBN: 978-1-78282-259-2 (hardcover)
ISBN: 978-1-78282-260-8 (softcover)

http://www.leonaur.com

Publisher's Notes

Contents

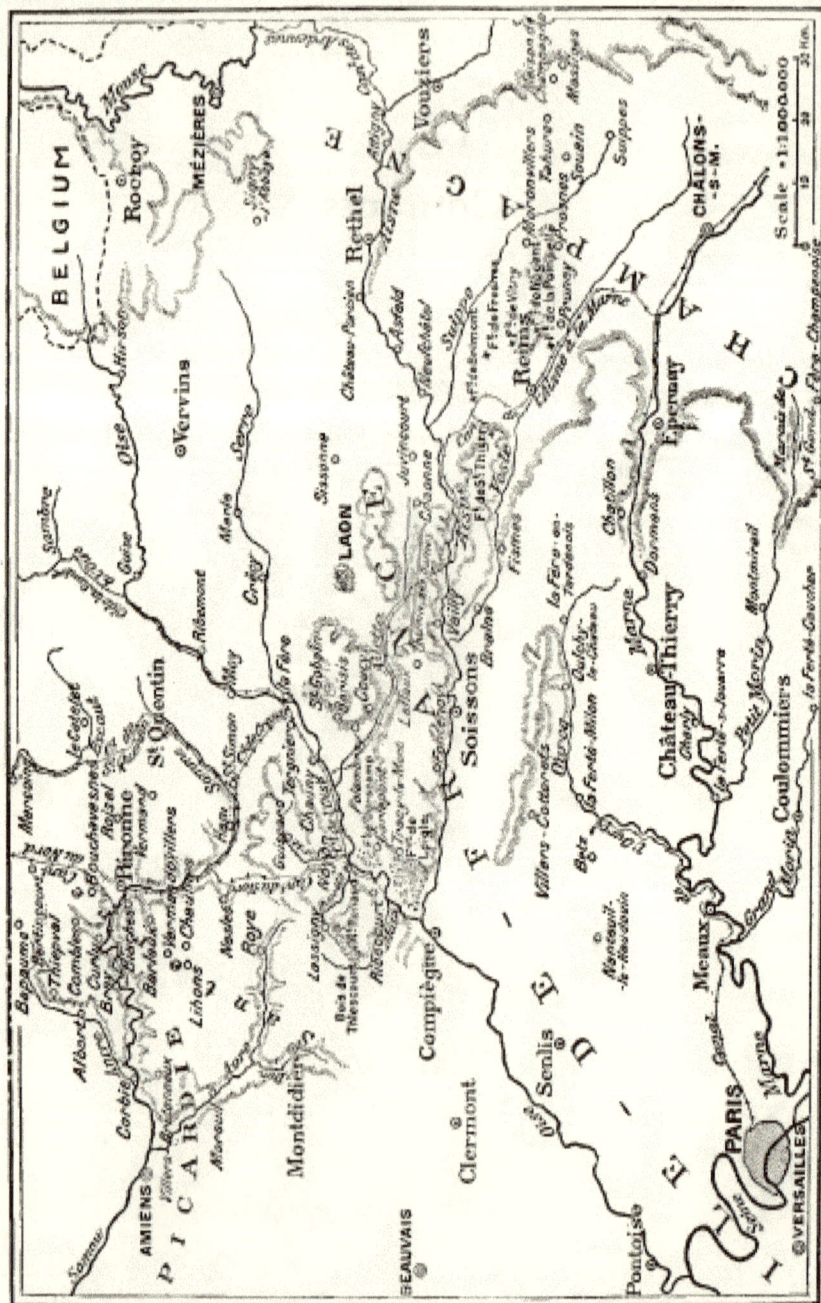

BELGIUM

Meuse

Rocroy

MÉZIÈRES

Vervins

Oise

Serre

Marle

Guise

Ribemont

St. Quentin

PICARDIE

AMIENS

Somme

Bapaume

Albert

Corbie

Combles

Thiepval

Bertangles

Péronne

Ham

Roye

Montdidier

Clermont

Senlis

BEAUVAIS

Pontoise

PARIS

VERSAILLES

Marne

Meaux

Coulommiers

Château-Thierry

Montmirail

la Ferté-Gaucher

Soissons

LAON

Villers-Cotterets

Compiègne

la Fère

Crépy

Oise

Aisne

Reims

Épernay

CHÂLONS-S-M.

Marne

Rethel

Vouziers

Mézières

Suippes

Château-Porcien

ARGONNE

Scale 1:1,000,000

10   20   30 Kil.

Dedicated to
Major–General Adelbert Cronkhite
Who Commanded Successively and Successfully
The Eightieth Division
And the Ninth and Sixth Army Corps
A. E. F.
For Whom as a Soldier
The Writer Entertains the Highest
Admiration
And for Whom as a Man
He Cherishes a Warm Affection

AND IT WAS NOT A DREAM!

Preface

Cantigny, Château Thierry, and the Counter-Offensive of July, 1918, the last commonly known as the Second Battle of the Marne, were the three operations in which American troops may be said to have made their initial appearance in battle in the Great War. Cooperating with the forces of the Allies, they first assisted them in checking the advance of the Germans and then in hurling the enemy back from the Marne across the Ourcq and Vesle. The successful operations in which they engaged during the critical days of June and July, 1918, marked the transition of the Allies from the defensive to the offensive and the turn of the tide of victory in favour of the Allies. The title selected for the following narrative is,, therefore, significantly appropriate.

In the preparation of this work I feel that I have had peculiar advantages. As a member of the Historical Section of the General Staff of the American Expeditionary Forces for a number of months after the Armistice, I not only had access to the archives at General Headquarters and came in contact with many of the leaders in the war, but I was enabled to visit every battlefield of which I have written and to make careful studies of them before time had obliterated the evidence which must henceforth be lacking to the historian. Furthermore, I had the great honour and good fortune to be attached to the French and British Armies in the Vosges and Flanders, respectively, before engaging in campaign with my own command, and later of serving with my own command while attached to the British Army in Picardy. The experience of the War thus gained, coupled with that of an active participation in the St. Mihiel and Meuse-Argonne campaigns, enabled me, I believe, to acquire a broader viewpoint than I might have had with more restricted opportunities.

In justice to our gallant and indomitable Allies who bore the brunt of the war and denied the Central Allies the ultimate victory while we were preparing to assist in attaining it, I have been careful to avoid the all too common error of overrating our physical contribution to the result. However great the moral effect of our participation in the fighting on the Marne may have been, and it is hard to overestimate that effect, the time has come when in justice to ourselves as well as to our Allies we should view the events of the war sanely, and endeavour to see them in their true perspective. Surely the truth is glorious enough, and there is no cause for our pride to suffer at its telling.

I am conscious of many grave defects in my work and claim for it the sole virtue that it is one of the first attempts to set forth concisely the facts about the momentous events which it purports to describe. In no instance have I sought to substitute mere rhetoric for figures, and I have purposely left the "human interest" to others in the belief that there is a large class of serious readers who now desire the unadorned truth.

To Brigadier-General Oliver L. Spaulding, Chief of the Historical Section, and to Major R. M. Johnston, his able assistant, formerly Professor of History at Harvard, I am indebted for much assistance in the course of my studies, and to Major Lincoln MacVeagh of the Historical Section for much valuable advice and criticism, and for most material assistance in the preparation of the book, including the reading and revision of the manuscript.

Jennings C. Wise.

Richmond, Va.,
November 11, 1919.

CHAPTER ONE

The Taking of Cantigny

1: PRELIMINARY

The Allied line as it stood after the first German offensive of 1918 swept westward from Reims, left Soissons and Compiègne to the south, turned north at Cantigny, and passed east of Amiens and Ypres to the North Sea. It thus embraced the important position of Montdidier. A tremendous blow had just been delivered to the British Army. The German offensive of March was by far the greatest effort that had yet been made by the enemy, and the Allied High Command, which had been hard pressed to arrest the victorious onrush of the Germans, had, in fact, accomplished this only by transferring to the British front large French reinforcements, thereby greatly weakening the front held by the French Army. During the succeeding brief period of general stabilization, it was clearly foreseen that the German High Command would resume the offensive. It was known that the enemy was gathering strength for another great effort. But the exact quarter in which the blow would fall could not be foretold.

Meanwhile, General, now Marshal, Foch had been made *generalissimo* of all the Allied forces, and his first care had been to establish the Allied line as firmly as possible throughout its wide extent, and especially in those quarters which appeared to offer the greatest temptation to the enemy.

His conception of meeting a renewed offensive did not embody a mere passive defence. Believing that the enemy would make a great thrust toward Paris west of Compiègne, he undertook preparations looking to a counter-attack by the First French Army from the west against the enemy's right flank.

At this time the front from Amiens past Compiègne and Soissons was held by the First, Third, Tenth, and Sixth French Armies in order named from left to right, comprising the army group of General Fayolle. Confronting this group of armies were the Second, Eighteenth, and Seventh German Armies, in the order named from west to east, commanded by von der Marwitz, von Hutier, and von Boehn, respectively. The contemplated counter-offensive by the First French Army involved the massing of an adequate force in the Montdidier sector. In view of the necessity for utilizing a large part of the French reserves on the British front, the problem of organising a sufficient force for the counter-attack was a serious one. Nor was the American Army able at this critical hour—just one year after the entry of the United States into the war—to contribute largely to the aggregate effective strength of the Allies. Nevertheless, fortunately, it was able to participate with an effect disproportionate to its numerical strength—with a political effect far exceeding in value its mere military contribution of the hour.

From the day that American troops arrived in France, the American High Command had been engaged in a desperate contest to maintain the American Expeditionary Forces as a separate and distinct combatant army. It was in vain that the French and British Governments urged the absorption of the American combat units by their own armies. Again and again they put forth this proposal in one form or another, but always to no avail. It would be unprofitable to consider here the two sides of the question involved. There was, no doubt, much reason on either side. Suffice it to say that the American view, which is now generally believed to have been the better, prevailed, and, when the crisis of the war arrived, General Pershing, without hesitating, but without receding in any respect from the principles which he had consistently adhered to, was able on March 28th to place at the disposal of Marshal Foch a number of American combat divisions.

At least one of these divisions was available for immediate use—the 1st U. S. Division, with Major-General Robert L. Bullard commanding,—which was at the time occupying a quiet sector north of Toul. It was accordingly called upon and placed in the Montdidier sector north of Paris, where on May 28th, 1918, it took the little town of Cantigny in an operation now seen to be of an importance out of all proportion to its obvious local character. It was in fact an operation which preluded the participation in the war of the Americans as a separate military force. It gave proof to the Central Allies of the rap-

12

idly developing military power of the United States, and its prestige strengthened the hand of General Pershing in his efforts to form an American Army in France.

2: THE 1ST DIVISION

No narrative of the Cantigny operation would be complete without at least a brief account of the character and the prior service of the troops engaged in it. These troops composed the 1st U. S. Division, which by official designation, length of service, and the variety and importance of its services, may be said to have been in the Spring of 1918 the premier division of the American Expeditionary Forces.

Commanded by Major-General William L. Sibert, the 1st Division had been transported to France in June and July, 1917, composing at the time the greater part of the original American Expeditionary Forces. Assembled in the Gondrecourt area the infantry of the division immediately undertook its training with the 69th French Division, General Monroe commanding, while the artillery was assigned to the separate training area of Valdahon under the direction of Lieutenant-Colonel Maître of the French Army.

It was at this time, too, that, by an odd flip of fortune, the artillery came under the special tutelage of the great-great-grandson of the Marquis de Lafayette in the person of Lieutenant-Colonel de Chambrun. Inspired with an inherited attachment to the American Army, possessed of the deepest personal interest in it by reason of long association with American affairs, and endowed with no ordinary abilities as a soldier, the Comte de Chambrun rendered a service of inestimable value.

After undergoing a most vigorous course of instruction, the division entered the quiet sector of Sommervillier in Lorraine, where from October 21st to November 20th its infantry and artillery battalions were attached for instructional purposes to the corresponding units of the 18th French Division. While occupying its sector the infantry was raided by a small force of the enemy in front of Burges, and suffered the first American casualties in the war.

Upon the conclusion of its initial instruction in the trenches the division was again assembled in the Gondrecourt area and there underwent the most gruelling training. Words are inadequate to describe the hardships sustained by officers and men alike during this period—hardships that were inevitable, however unnecessary many of them are now seen to have been. Indeed, it was but natural that the division

His Calvary: For the Salvation of the World

should have suffered from the disadvantage of being the first American division in more than the sense of its official designation. But the hardships to which it was subjected, useless or otherwise, the experiments that were ruthlessly tried upon it, the inexperience of officers and men, and the unusual severities of the winter, only sufficed to temper more highly the steel of which its spirit was composed, and to inure its physical being to the worst ordeals that more active operations might impose.

Those were the bitter days of a second "Valley Forge," when men marched over frozen roads and through the snow, ill-clad, and barefooted. A serious shortage in almost everything essential to the proper equipment, clothing, and housing of the troops had existed from the first, but no man complained. Instead of improving with the passage of time, conditions seemed to grow worse as the days grew colder and the snows more frequent. The pages of military history devoted to the record of the American Army will never do justice to the men who underwent training in France during the winter of 1917-18. Never has the history of war recorded a finer spirit than they displayed.

Nevertheless it would be absurd to say that the men who displayed this spirit were consciously inspired by exalted motives. In their hours of reflection, if such existed, they may have dimly perceived, as they probably at all times felt, the justice of the Allied cause. But in their mental attitude and bearing there was no suggestion of the Crusader. Their inspiration was simply that of keen competition, dear to all Americans. They were fighting against the mighty German Army, side by side with the British and the French and the latter's justly famed Colonials; and they were determined to be foremost in the field. They were thoroughly aware that the world, grown critical with impatience, awaited their appearance in battle. They viewed their part as that of fresh substitutes in a great game in which after long delay their chance had come.

On January 15th, 1918, the 1st Division took over the Ansauville sector north of Toul, relieving the 1st Moroccan Division and functioning for the first time as a complete combat unit in the line. The command of the division, at first exercised by General Monroe, of the 69th French Division in the sector on the right, passed on February 5th to Major-General Robert L. Bullard, who had succeeded General Sibert.

It was well that the division was to receive so soon its first independent war experience. Raided by the enemy on March 1st with few resulting casualties, it conducted (on March 11th) two counter-raids, the success of which served to establish a high morale and a sense of superiority over the enemy on the part of the troops. The orders which were received shortly afterwards, transferring the division to the Montdidier sector north of Paris, at the most important and critical point on the front of the First French Army, with which it was to engage in the proposed counteroffensive, found it already a seasoned and experienced division.

Relieved in the Ansauville sector between March 30th and April 3rd by the 26th U. S. Division, the 1st Division was entrained in the neighbourhood of Toul and moved between April 6th and 9th to the vicinity of Méru, northeast of Paris, whence it marched to Chaumont-en-Vexin. Receiving a hasty and belated training in open warfare in the latter area between April 7th and 16th, it marched on the 17th, 18th, and 19th to Anneuil, Nivillers, and Froissy, and on the night of April 20th-21st was placed under the orders of the Sixth Corps of the First French Army, The following night it commenced the relief of the 162nd French Division in the Cantigny sector, immediately west of Montdidier, finally taking over the command of the sector on the morning of the 25th.

The line which it held extended approximately three and a half kilometres from a point north of Mesnil St. Georges in front of Le Cardonnois to a point west of Cantigny in front of Villers-Tournelle. Though the American position generally overlooked the German position, the latter possessed especially good observation from the high point of Grivesnes, about three kilometres northwest of Cantigny. Likewise from Cantigny itself there was good observation over the approaches to the town, rendering all movement within the sector forward of the line Mesnil St. Georges-Villers-Tournelle impracticable by day. Having been in occupation of the position less than three weeks the French had been unable to construct trenches or shelters, or even to erect wire entanglements along their front.

Division Headquarters and Headquarters 1st Artillery Brigade were established at Mesnil St. Firmin about six kilometres from the hostile line, with the 1st and 2nd Brigade Headquarters at Serevillers and Mesnil St. Firmin, respectively. The 1st Infantry Brigade occupied the front line, with the 16th and 18th Infantry abreast, the former on the right, while the remainder of the division was stationed in the rear of the sector in the vicinity of Froissy. Two battalions of infantry of the 2nd Brigade, however, were posted in close reserve at Rocquencourt

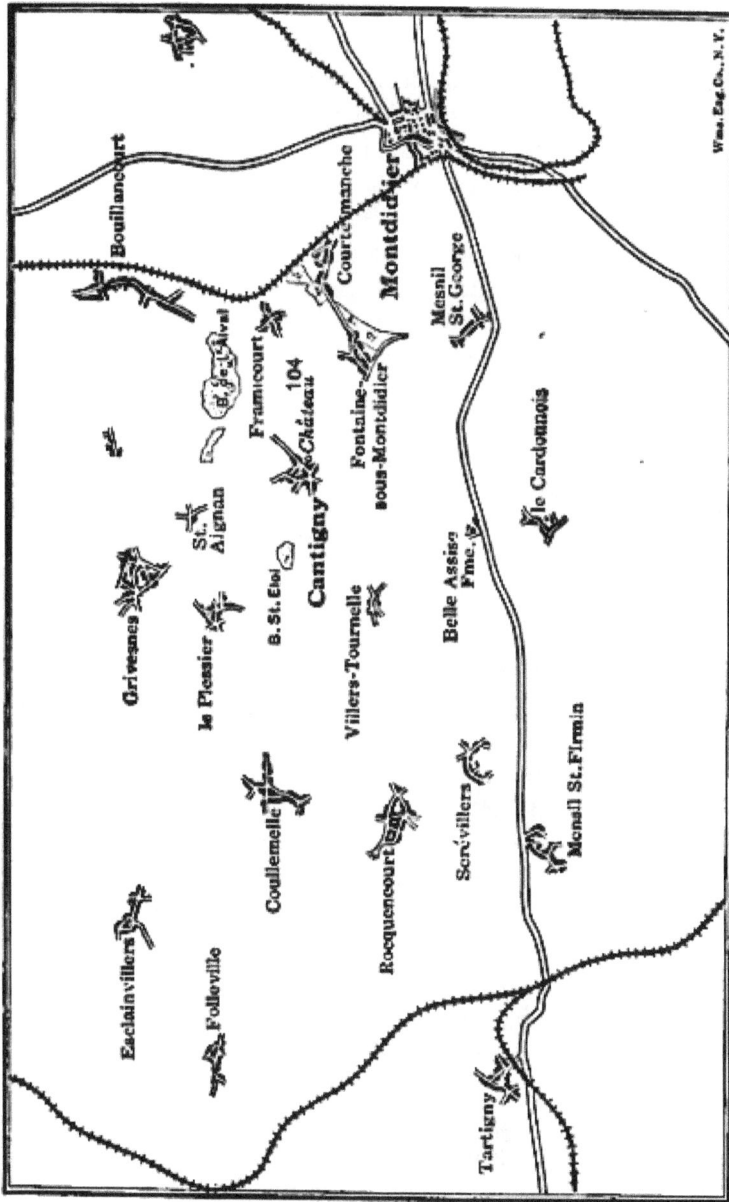

CANTIGNY

and Mesnil St. Firmin, while the 1st Field Artillery Brigade was reinforced by a battalion of French 75 mm. guns.

Throughout the latter part of April and May the hostile artillery was very active and annoying. Nevertheless, over two thousand men were engaged nightly in consolidating the sector. First, second, and third line positions were prepared, a complete system of trenches opened, and the necessary dugouts and shelters constructed. The amount of labour imposed by this comprehensive work was enormous, and all of it was rendered more difficult by the excellent observation which the enemy possessed and his persistent harassing with high explosive and gas shells. The casualties from gas alone were large.

One who has not actually been present within such a sector can scarcely appreciate the travail which life therein imposes upon its tenants. Tasks which under ordinary conditions would seem small indeed become undertakings of extreme difficulty and assume enormous proportions. Work which on a map would appear most simple to an engineer is in fact all but impossible of accomplishment through the dangerous exposure of the working parties. In the Cantigny sector there was likewise the difficulty of transporting material over fire-swept roads ceaselessly harassed by hostile artillery. Every cross-road, every trail, was systematically searched, and every ravine or area which afforded natural cover from direct fire was kept filled with the poisonous vapours of the enemy's gas shells. Indeed, the problem of transporting water, rations, and ammunition to the forward areas was a serious and laborious one in itself, not to speak of the construction of trenches and dugouts.

Under such conditions, though men do manage to live, and even the casualties prove to be more annoying than numerous, life tends to become a mere struggle to survive, which, without the constant prod on energetic and intelligent direction, soon degenerates into an existence devoid of all interest in the future and inspired with but one hope—the hope of living. Under the abnormal and unremitting strain to which they are subjected the keenest minds often grow dull. The most essential tasks appear to them unnecessary—mere useless burdens. The most obvious precautions are neglected or wholly omitted. All sense of proportion is lost, and not only men's minds but men's souls at times seem to shrivel up and die.

Some idea of the severity of the ordeal through which the division passed while in occupation of the Cantigny sector may be formed from the total of its casualties. Though the losses involved in the actual taking and holding of Cantigny, which is to be described, did not exceed a thousand, its losses between April 25th and July 5th were forty-nine officers and eight hundred and four men killed, eighty-one officers and two thousand one hundred and eighty-two men wounded, and fifty-three officers and two thousand one hundred and thirty-six men gassed, or an aggregate of one hundred and eighty-three officers and five thousand one hundred and twenty-two men. Most of these losses were suffered during the latter part of April and the month of May.

But the division was fortunate in possessing a staff of unusual capacity. Carefully selected, and with the eyes of the military world fixed upon it, that staff was fully alive to its grave responsibilities. It addressed itself, accordingly, to the tremendous task before it with the vigour of fresh enthusiasm. From the very first the division, officers and men alike, was inspired with the hope of an early advance. Brought to the west for the direct purpose of engaging in an offensive operation, it was carefully led to regard the hostile position which it confronted as its immediate goal, and the defences which it was called on to prepare with so much toil as but the means to an end, and not as the end itself. Carefully studying the life within the opposite sector the staff became surprisingly familiar with the enemy's habits, and was able to determine when and where the most damage to him could be wrought. Alternative routes of supply, watering points, and assembling places were harassed as soon as it was believed that the enemy had become habituated through necessity to their use, and by this means his normal losses were increased. Furthermore, his morale was lowered and the spirit of the division itself correspondingly increased by the sense of American superiority which the practice created.

The particular staff officer upon whom devolved the responsibility for the direction of the harassing fire, made it a point to study the habits of the enemy's horse transport. Every possible locality where animals might be watered was considered along with all the probabilities in the case. Then after repeatedly harassing some of these points and carefully avoiding others, the fire was switched on a certain night to the watering points which it was reasoned the enemy had through necessity come to use. The trick produced the most telling results. With prompt acknowledgment, indeed, the Germans attempted the following night to use it against the Americans.

Such incidents were not typical of the artillery only. The whole division entered upon its life in the trenches with no idea of making

19

Two Friends: French poilu and American officer

them its permanent abode. The inertia neither of despair nor of satisfaction with the *status quo* settled upon it. Nor was it in its nature to rest content with the conditions of stabilization. Its spirit was that of open warfare—the warfare of movement. It had witnessed the inadequacy of the old methods. Rightly or wrongly it did not believe that it was necessary to adhere to those methods till numerical superiority, inclined to the Allies.

3: THE TAKING OF CANTIGNY

On April 30th the 45th French Division on the left of the 1st U. S. Division was relieved by the 152nd French Division, and on May 7th the 162nd French Division on the right of the 1st was relieved by the 60th French Division. On May 5th the Tenth French Corps replaced the Sixth, to which the 1st U. S. Division had hitherto been attached. Measures for the execution of the proposed counter-attack were energetically pressed. Behind the division were emplaced an enormous number of French batteries, including one hundred and thirty-two 75 mm. guns, thirty-six 155 mm. howitzers, sixteen 220 mm. and 280 mm. howitzers, and twenty-four 58 mm., six 150 mm., and four 240 mm. trench mortars, or over two hundred pieces of artillery.

Every detail was arranged for the counter-attack, including the issue of the regimental orders. The taking of Cantigny was determined upon as a preliminary measure with the purpose of depriving the enemy of the excellent observation and of the other advantages which that salient position afforded him. It is not too much to say that its possession was essential to either side if a surprise attack in force were to be delivered in the region of Montdidier. Somewhat lower than the higher ridges within the American sector, the Cantigny plateau tilted like a shelf toward the south, with the town resting at the middle of its forward edge. About four kilometres in width from east to west it screened the country in its rear where excellent positions for artillery and communications for the movement of troops and supplies existed. It was necessary for the Allies to advance their artillery from the zone of Mesnil St. Firmin to the line Cantigny-Fontaine-sous-Montdidier-Mesnil St. Georges in order to render this terrain impracticable for the massing of reserves.

The task of taking the Cantigny plateau naturally fell to the 1st U. S. Division in the sector opposite the position. On May 14th-15th the 2nd Infantry Brigade had relieved the 1st Infantry Brigade in the front line. The 28th Infantry was, therefore, selected to make the attack, and on the night of May 22nd-23rd was withdrawn to the area of Maisoncelle-St. Eusoye about twenty kilometres in rear for special training. From the time of the division's appearance in the line the enemy had held the supremacy of the air, though the French planes had been most active, so that secrecy of preparations was the very essence of any success that might be obtained. In the rear area every detail of the attack, as planned by the Division Staff, was thoroughly rehearsed in conjunction with the 5th Group of French Assault Tanks, consisting of three batteries of four tanks each. A detachment of French flamethrowers was also attached to the regiment.

On May 27th the Germans renewed their offensive, this time against the thin French line on the Chemin des Dames. On the same day at 6:30 a.m. the enemy made three small raids along the front of the 1st U. S. Division following a very heavy bombardment with high explosive and gas shells. Although he succeeded in penetrating the Bois Fontaine and the zone of Belle Assise to its left, he was driven back and his trenches in the Bois Allonge occupied. Only two American prisoners were taken, in exchange for four German prisoners, and less than two hundred casualties, including eight killed, were suffered by the division. These raids failed utterly to discover the designs for the American attack of the following day.

Between April 26th and May 16th, inclusive, the German line had been held by the 30th Division on the left and the 25th Reserve Division on the right. On the latter date the 30th Division was relieved by the 82nd Reserve Division. The position assailed by the 28th Infantry was held on the morning of May 28th by two regiments of the 82nd Reserve Division, namely the 271st and 272nd Reserve Regiments, the former occupying the town itself. The 271st was not an especially good regiment, and after the loss of its position it was severely criticised by the German corps commander for the feeble resistance it had opposed to the Americans. The 272nd Reserve Regiment held the northern outskirts of the town and the terrain to the north. Both the 271st and 272nd Reserve Regiments had one battalion in forward positions, one in support in the Bois Framicourt and Bois de Lalval, respectively, and one at rest twelve kilometres or more from the front line. Thus it is seen that no very formidable force confronted the 1st U. S. Division. The German infantry, however, was strongly supported at all times by the artillery.

As was to be expected, the staff-work on the part of the 1st Division in connection with the Cantigny operation was excellent in all respects. In fact, the precision as to details which its work discloses makes its preparations and orders on this occasion models of their kind. The objective designated was a line one kilometre beyond the village of Cantigny, extending from the region of St. Aignan on the west along the forward edge of the wood northeast of the village to point 104 overlooking Courtemanche and the ravine leading along the eastern face of the plateau. Upon reaching the objective a new line of trenches was to be rapidly organised under the cover of the concentrated fire of the artillery along the entire corps front. There was to be a heavy artillery preparation of one hour before the attack, followed by a rolling barrage which was to fall on the enemy at 6:45 a.m. and progress at the rate of one hundred meters in two minutes. The divisions on the flanks were to support the attack in every way possible from their positions, while the 152nd French Division on the left was to maintain liaison with the left of the 28th Infantry.

The attack was to be made on a front of twenty-two hundred metres by three battalions in line, the left and centre battalions with three, and the right battalion with two companies in the front line. The right of the centre battalion was to advance straight upon and through the village of Cantigny, while the left of the battalion was to approach the village from the west and north, a group of tanks preceding this battalion. The left battalion, in liaison with the 152nd French Division on the left and the centre battalion on the right, was to proceed to the objective in the zone of St. Aignan. The two companies of the right battalion, advancing east, were to insure the cleaning up of the southern portion of Cantigny and maintain liaison on the right. The companies in regimental reserve were to conform to the front line battalions, one moving to the ravine southwest of Cantigny after the attack had commenced.

On the night of May 26th-27th one battalion of the 28th Infantry was brought up in trucks from the rear training area to relieve a battalion of the 18th Infantry in line. The following night the remainder of the regiment was brought up and by 3:30 a.m., on May 28th, was in position ready for the attack. The left battalion was posted with three companies in the front line five hundred meters east and northeast of Bois St. Éloi, and with one company in support in the wood itself, relieving in this zone one company of the 114th Regiment, 152nd French Division, and one company of the 18th Infantry. The right battalion with three companies relieved one company of the 18th Infantry in the Bois de Cantigny and one company in the vicinity of

the Bois Suisse, taking over the line that extended from the western edge of the former through the Bois Suisse to a point one hundred meters north of the Bois Carré. One company of this battalion was posted in the Bois des Glands de Villers as regimental reserve, while two companies of the third battalion were posted north of Villers-Tournelle and in the western part of the Bois de Cantigny as a special regimental reserve which was not to be used without the authority of the brigade commander. A company of machine guns was attached to each of the two assault battalions; and a company of engineers, the twelve French tanks, and the platoon of French flame-throwers, with which the regiment had trained, were distributed along the line.

The regiment advanced in three lines according to schedule. The first line leaned hard upon the barrage, while the second line closed upon the first so that all elements would be two hundred yards from the old front line at H, plus 10 minutes, and thus avoid being caught by a counter-barrage.[1] The third line conformed to the advance. No Man's Land was crossed without incident. No counter-barrage fell, and the enemy infantry failed to react at the proper moment when the American barrage lifted. By 7:20 a.m. the objective was reached, and immediately automatic rifle groups were pushed forward to shell holes along the line of surveillance to cover the consolidation. Meantime the resistance line was consolidated with trenches and wire, while three strong-points were organised along the third line, one about two hundred meters east of the *château* in Cantigny, one in the woods at the north-eastern exit of the village, and the third at the cemetery to the north. In this work the company of engineers proved of great assistance, while the French flame-throwers inspired terror among the enemy during the process of cleaning up the position. The French tanks were operated with complete success and without loss of materiel. The hostile position was penetrated to an extreme depth of about sixteen hundred meters with a loss to the division not exceeding a total of thirty. The entire garrison was either killed or captured, two hundred and seventy-five dead being counted. Prisoners to the number of two hundred and twenty-five, including five officers, were taken.

It was not until about noon that the enemy's artillery became active. Having definitely located the American line by that time, for the

---

1. Note: "H-hour" was the phrase used by the Americans to designate the moment of attack, as the better known phrase " Zero hour" was used by the British. Similarly "D-day" was used to designate the day of attack.

next seventy-two hours the enemy subjected it to a terrific bombardment with high explosive and gas shells. Large calibre guns were employed, and machine-gun fire also became intense. At 7 30 a.m. a feeble counterattack by a small force had been attempted without success from the Bois Fontaine, and at 5:10 p.m. a similar vain effort was made from the western tip of the Bois Framicourt. The Americans took every precaution. During the night of May 28th-29th two companies of the 18th Infantry in reserve reinforced the line. One battalion of the 18th Infantry was posted at the southwest corner of the Bois des Glands, and another in the vicinity of Villers-Tournelle, where they were assembled in readiness throughout the night.

At 6 a.m. and 7 a.m. the following morning, the enemy launched two small counter-attacks both of which, like the two of the preceding day, were broken up by artillery and rifle fire. At 5:45 p.m., on the 29th, a stronger attack was delivered upon the left of the 28th Infantry, which was driven back slightly in the region of St. Aignan, but this attack was also soon broken up and the line re-established. On the 30th, at 5:30 a.m., the enemy made a seventh and final effort to recover the lost ground.

Preceded by a heavy artillery preparation, with 210 mm., 150 mm., and 77 mm. guns, a fairly large force—probably a battalion of infantry—came forward in two waves from the Lalval wood under the cover of a barrage. This attack met with no success whatever, being brought under machine-gun and artillery fire in its initial stages. This counter-attack, like the one on the previous evening, was no doubt made by one of the enemy's reserve battalions.

After the morning of May 30th, the activity of the enemy lessened. This enabled the greater part of the 28th Infantry to be relieved by the 16th Infantry on the night of the 30th-31st, the relief being completed the following night. It was now apparent that the enemy did not possess the present strength to wrest back the position which the Americans had seized from him almost without loss in the operation itself. But the casualties sustained by the Americans on the afternoons of the 28th, on the 29th, and on the morning of the 30th, were severe, including thirteen officers and one hundred and eighty-six men killed, thirty-one officers and six hundred and twenty-one men wounded, two hundred men gassed, and one officer and fifteen men missing, or a total of forty-five officers and one thousand and twenty-two men. The great majority of these casualties were suffered by the 28th Infantry.

4: Consolidation

As soon as Cantigny had been seized, the 1st U. S. Division undertook with energy the organisation of its new position. On the night of May 31st-June 1st it relieved the right half of the 152nd French Division on its left in the quarters of Mocador, St. Aignan, and Grivesnes. By June 9th the necessary redistribution of the division over an increased front of six kilometres was complete. The northern sub-sector of the division was held by the 1st Brigade, and the southern sub-sector by the 2nd Brigade, with headquarters at Foileville and Mesnil St. Firmin, respectively; while the 18th, 16th, 28th, and 26th Infantry in line in the order named from left to right held the zones of Esclainvillers, Coullemelle, Villers-Tournelle, and. Broyes, respectively.

On June 4th, Division Headquarters moved to Tartigny. The great mass of French artillery which had been assigned to the support of the 1st Division was withdrawn to other quarters, owing to the German offensive of May 27th-June 6th. Only the divisional artillery remained, but this increased its activities with an average daily expenditure of approximately twenty-two thousand rounds of ammunition. The enemy's artillery likewise continued its ceaseless harassing fire and his bombing planes an undiminished activity. The morale of the division, however, remained at a high pitch. The sector continued to be a strenuous one, but no counter-attacks were experienced, though they were expected on the nights both of June 7th and June 8th. The enemy's offensive operations at this time reached only as far west as Montdidier.

Without regard to what was occurring on other fronts, a complete program of work looking to the thorough consolidation of the sector was now undertaken. First, second, and third lines of resistance were completed, and the division was disposed on these in great depth with a strongly held outpost zone. All forward units remained under orders to fight in their positions. The third line battalions were posted west of the Paris-Amiens railroad, nine kilometres or more to the west.

Due to the enemy's diminished power of observation and the bettered positions of the troops, the daily casualties now decreased, and conditions within the sector generally became more tolerable. Only two inferior German divisions confronted the entire extended front of the 1st Division—the 1st Reserve and the 82nd Reserve Divisions opposite its left and right, respectively, the 30th Division having been withdrawn for use elsewhere.[2]

---

2. Two German divisions, like the corresponding French and British units, were about the equivalent in numbers of one U. S. division.

THE "YANKS" IN FRONT OF FISMES

On May 27th, the Germans had launched their third great offensive of 1918, and had broken the Allied line between Soissons and
Reims. On May 31st, elements of the 3rd U. S. Division had been
thrust into the line at Château Thierry, and on June 2nd the 2nd U.
S. Division had formed a line across the Paris road west of the town.
Who shall estimate the effect of the glowing reports of Cantigny upon
the American troops at Château Thierry during the critical days of
early June? Near Montdidier the Americans, placed in the line at a
most vital point, had not only held their own but had actually seized
an important position which the enemy was loath to give up. Can one
doubt that the spirit of emulation inspired their comrades in barring
what appeared to be an open route to Paris?

5: Conclusion

Anxious days, never to be forgotten, succeeded the taking of Cantigny. The great wave of the German offensive surged past and hourly
threatened to engulf the little town. Far from its rear came the rumble
of battle as the enemy pressed on toward the Marne. It seemed almost as if the 1st Division were isolated and forgotten. Breathlessly it
awaited from hour to hour the tidings which sifted along the lines—
tidings which reached it, on at least one occasion, with dark forebodings of disaster, when a carrier pigeon fell lifeless within its lines bearing a German despatch that the Marne had been crossed by German
troops.

But men breathed more freely as the attack extended westward
along the Aisne. In the very neighbourhood of Montdidier it was
successfully resisted by the First and Third French Armies, north of
Compiègne and west of Soissons. Finally it was checked altogether
between the Aisne and the Ourcq by the flank attack of Mangin's
Tenth Army on June 11th. Then, as the smoke of the great battle
which had lasted a fortnight cleared away, the old hope of victory
revived with more than the old life. For in the feats of American arms
at Cantigny and at Château Thierry romance once more seemed to
have entered upon the tragic stage of war.

Discount as one will such an intangible factor in the ultimate victory, the truth is it had a most material effect upon the battle lines
from Switzerland to the sea—an effect which inspired on the one side
as it discouraged on the other. In every dugout, on every sentry post in
Flanders, along the Somme, in Champagne and the Vosges, the weary
outposts of the Allies whispered of a victory that seemed nearer with

the advent of the American soldiers, and generously exaggerated the glory of their deeds.

Still another brilliant episode—the taking of Vaux on July 1st by the 2nd U. S. Division—was soon heralded to the world, followed by the official statement on July 4th that over a million American troops had been landed in France. Were these indeed the equivalent of forty divisions like those which had fought at Cantigny and Château Thierry; and if so, of eighty French or British divisions refreshed from war weariness and reinspired with hope? It was not strange that in the British Isles, in France, in Italy, in far-off Rumania, in the remotest corners of the earth, men should have vied in that hour in celebrating the national anniversary of the United States.

Within the 1st Division the celebration took a novel and peculiar form. During the morning horse shows were held by the brigades and a salute of forty-eight guns—one for each State of the Union—was fired across the hostile line. That night five thousand gas shells, the first concentration of these projectiles attempted by the Americans, were hurled into the enemy's position opposite Cantigny.

Between the 5th and 8th of July the division was relieved by the 152nd and 166th French Divisions, before the enraged enemy could devise some form of retaliation for the gas attack. On July 5th the orders were received that withdrew it to the rear area of Beauvais. There it was to train in open warfare in preparation for the great counter-offensive of July 18th. But the record of its brilliant services in those operations comprises a separate chapter in the history of the American Expeditionary Forces in France.

The original military purpose for which the division was transferred to the Cantigny sector was never fulfilled. The contemplated counter-attack was not delivered. Viewed from the standpoint of the Allied High Command, the mere taking of Cantigny, though an important minor operation, was a local one. Indeed of such small note was it in a military way that had it been carried out by French or British troops their success would scarcely have been remarked in the rapid train of events of that crucial hour. Nor was it notable by reason of any especial difficulty in the operation itself. Certainly there was no disparity of force in favour of the enemy. On the contrary, the assailants possessed an undoubted superiority in that respect.

It is to the political and moral significance of the event that we must look if we are to appreciate its full importance. Politically it was of far-reaching effect. There is even ground for the belief that it was for political reasons pure and simple that the 1st U. S. Division, rather than some more experienced French or British unit, was committed to the line at the place and hour chosen. The timing of the play was exact, if the appearance of the American troops was to have its maximum psychological effect. As a result, the taking of Cantigny possesses the importance of a major operation. It stimulated the weakened pulse of the Allied armies. It stirred and exhilarated the American people at home, for whom it became an episode of epic proportions. It marks the beginning of the war's end.

CHAPTER TWO

Château Thierry

1: PRELIMINARY

The political demise of Kerensky on November 5th, 1917, and the complete collapse of Russia as a military ally of Great Britain, France, and Italy made it possible in the Spring of 1917 for the Central Allies to abandon the defensive attitude which circumstances had imposed upon them during the past two years. With what appeared to be a military preponderance on the western front, their first great offensive of March 21st was directed to the severance of the British and French armies by cutting in the region of the Somme the lines of communication leading northward from Paris. After the failure to gain a decision by this drive, a second offensive was launched in April crippling the British in the region of the Lys but again falling short of a decisive victory. The latter offensive left the Central Allies confronted with a serious crisis in their man-power situation.

So great a number of effectives had been expended on the Somme and the Lys that in May the crisis became not only military but political as well. The German High Command could not fail to see that a decision must be obtained at once if it were to be obtained at all. Ludendorff could not expect to retain much longer the numerical superiority he possessed, assuming that he still possessed it after his first two exhausting efforts. With the eventual appearance of the American Army upon the stage, that superiority would most certainly be lost.

We have seen, in our discussion of Cantigny, that to meet the German offensive the Allies had been hard put to it, and that General, now Marshal, Foch, elevated to the supreme command of the Allied forces late in March, had been compelled to draw heavily upon the French Army to retrieve the situation north of the Somme. As a consequence the Allied line necessarily had been weakened, though generally in quarters which appeared to offer the least temptation to the enemy, and which were subjected to the least hostile pressure.

Among the weakened sectors was that best described as the Chemin des Dames. Consisting of a range of hills, running east and west a distance of forty kilometres, parallel with the Aisne, it had been taken by the French in April, 1917, at frightful cost. For a year it had stood as a bulwark for the Allies facing Laon and rendering more secure Compiègne, Soissons, and Reims along the Aisne and Vesle to the south.

Between the Aisne and Vesle, another range of hills lay east and west from Soissons to Reims—a distance of fifty kilometres. Farther south, a high, undulating plateau of farms and woodlands stretched thirty kilometres to the Marne, affording an excellent intervening defensive position along the Ourcq which lay midway between the Vesle and the Marne. A successful advance directly southward from the region of Laon would, therefore, entail upon the enemy the forcing of not one, but four successive lines of defence of great natural strength—the Chemin des Dames, the Aisne-Vesle line, the Ourcq, and the Marne. Indeed, so secure in comparison with other sectors did the Chemin des Dames seem in May that for a distance of forty kilometres between Vauxaillon and Cormicy the line was held by but three French and three exhausted British divisions.

Late in May the German mass of manoeuvre amounted to eighty-two divisions, those which had suffered most in the two previous offensives having had from five to eight weeks to recuperate. These reserves were known by the Allies to be distributed in rest areas in Picardy. Between Chauny on the west and Craonne on the east, confronting the Chemin des Dames, von Boehn's Seventh Army held the German line. In line from right to left was the Eighth Reserve Corps, composed of the 211th, 14th Reserve, and 241st Reserve Divisions; the Fifty-fourth Corps, composed of .the 6th Bavarian Reserve and 13th Landwehr Divisions; and the Fifteenth Bavarian Reserve Corps, composed of the 197th, 231st, and 103rd Divisions, with the 5th Guard Division in reserve behind it. No other German troops were assembled south of Laon.

On the other hand, opposing these nine German divisions were in line from left to right three corps of the Sixth French Army as follows: the Thirtieth French Corps, with the 55th, 19th, 2nd Colonial, and 151st Divisions in the front line supported by the 39th; the Eleventh

TANKS IN THE BATTLE (CHAMPAGNE)

French Corps, with the 64th, 21st, and 22nd Divisions supported by the 74th and 157th; and the Ninth British Corps, with the 50th, 8th, and 21st Divisions supported by the 25th. Ten Allied divisions, therefore, with four in support or close reserve, faced eight enemy divisions, supported by one division. The sense of security entertained by the Allied High Command seems to have been justified.

From the time General Foch assumed command late in March he expected the enemy to thrust toward Paris in the direction of Compiègne. In this belief he had fully prepared a counter-attack in the region of Montdidier for which every detail remained arranged throughout the month of May. But the uncertainty of war was once more to be demonstrated. The reserves for the proposed counter-operation were concentrated too far to the west when the third German offensive broke the Allied line to enable an attack to be launched with them upon the German right.

The break-through came east and not west of Compiègne, and was the result of very skilful manoeuvring on the part of the Germans. Within the sector of the Seventh German Army the headquarters of the First, Twenty-fifth Reserve, and Twenty-eighth Reserve Corps were quietly established in advance, and during the last few days before the attack six shock divisions were introduced from the areas of adjoining sectors, namely the 6th, 5th, 37th, 36th, and 10th Divisions from von Hutier's Eighteenth Army on the right, and the 113th Division from the reserve of the Seventeenth Army in the group of the Crown Prince on the left. By skilfully concealing the location of the newly arrived artillery and by moving the infantry reinforcements at night, the necessary secrecy of the concentration was fully preserved. Though as early as May 18th the American Staff had pointed out the possibility of an attack on the Chemin des Dames, the Allies were not definitely forewarned of the impending blow till the 26th, when whole battalions were observed advancing in the enemy's rear areas. The attack came on the 27th, and the surprise was virtually complete.

2: The Third German Offensive of 1918

At 1 a.m. on the 27th of May, the German artillery opened a bombardment even more severe than that of the 21st of March, though shorter in duration. At 4:30 a.m. the infantry advanced to the attack, meeting with immediate and complete success. So completely was the Allied line overwhelmed that within twenty-four hours the apex of the German advance penetrated nineteen kilometres, and reached a point about twelve kilometres from Fère-en-Tardenois on the Ourcq, midway between the Aisne and the Marne. In vain the hard-pressed Allied divisions sought to stay the onrush of the enemy during the next two days. Driven from position to position, they were so hotly pursued that an effective line of resistance could not be established as they fell back. On the 30th, disintegration set in to such an extent among the Allied troops that they were incapable of seriously opposing the crossing of the Ourcq in the region of Fère-en-Tardenois. Breaking through at this point the third line of natural defences, the enemy's columns pressed southward to the Marne as rapidly as they could march, hardly checked here and there by brave but isolated groups. The French artillery, continuing in action, fired by the map. But though from the Ourcq to the Marne it made itself persistently annoying to the enemy, it was unable to stay or even delay his advance to any great extent.

This sudden success probably exceeded the expectations of the German High Command, which found itself operating south of the Vesle on the 31st with the same fifteen divisions employed in the assault on the Chemin des Dames on the 27th. Crowded into the gap between Soissons and Reims which had resulted from the breakthrough, there was scarcely room for so large a force to manoeuvre effectively. The initial fighting and rapid pursuit of four days had imposed a great physical strain upon the troops, and the question of supply over the limited and crowded roads grew more complicated with each mile of advance. The momentum of the drive would of necessity expend itself soon, and continued progress southward, even though possible or unopposed, could lead to little more than the driving of the apex of the great salient a few miles beyond the Marne. On May 30th the first phase of the operation was nearing its close. The advance was reaching the "exploitation" stage, and the question was "what next?"

With the initiative still firmly theirs, despite the cramping of the troops in the lengthening salient, the Germans possessed a possible course of action in a turn to the southeast. About twenty kilometres to the east of their left flank lay the great north and south road which links Reims with Épernay. The cutting of this road would lead to the capture of Reims, together with much territory, and open the way for an advance along the line Épernay-Châlons with far-reaching consequences. Even a partial success towards these objectives would expose the flank of the Fourth French Army, which extended from Reims eastward to the Argonne Forest, and tend to make the Verdun salient untenable.

Undoubtedly the German General Staff had from the first considered the taking of Reims as one of its ultimate objectives, and had not up to this time seriously contemplated a lunge at Paris. When the Marne was in sight, however, it could not fail to appreciate the possibilities of a thrust toward the capital, either as a manoeuvre designed to facilitate the drive toward Reims, or as a separate operation in itself. Two routes were available for an advance to Paris, one from Soissons through Villers-Cotterêts and Dammartin, and one through Château Thierry and Meaux. Leaving the Reims operation for a future date, should the drive on Paris not yield decisive results, the Germans might swing to the southwest along these routes and endeavour to reach the greatest political prize of the war. Or they might be content with holding French reserves before the capital by a threatened push in that quarter and make their bid in another direction for immediate results of probably greater military value.

We are not yet able to say what influences determined the German choice. Strategy, considered from the military side alone, would seem to point to the southeast as the proper direction for the exploitation of the Third German Offensive. But strategy has its political side. Certain it is that, for whatever reason, beginning on the 30th of May when the central German column reached Fère-en-Tardenois, every division was deflected westward. The line of advance was henceforth not southeast or south, but southwest. The possibilities offered by a drive at the Reims-Épernay road were left for future consideration, and the German troops which ranged themselves during the succeeding days along the Marne were designed as a covering force only.

In the operation determined upon, it was planned to drive two salients into the Allied line, one toward Soissons, the other toward Château Thierry. This done, a much extended front directly menacing Paris from the northeast would remain to the assailants, and a continuation of their success would bring them within striking distance of Paris itself. The northernmost of these two local enemy problems, or the problem of the Soissons salient, need not be discussed at length. A glance at the map will show that the solution was intended to be along the stereotyped lines of a "pincers" attack. It was attempted on June 9th in the fourth German offensive of 1918, and decisively defeated by Mangin's Tenth Army two days later in the operations officially known as the Montdidier-Noyon Defensive, which extended over

German prisoner at work

the period from June 9th to June 13th. The southern problem was but a continuation of the third German offensive, which commenced May 27th and terminated June 5th. Officially known as the Aisne Defensive, the operations of the Allies during this period involved the employment of American troops as described in the sequel.

3: THE SITUATION ON MAY 31ST

Those who surrounded General Foch during the critical days of the Aisne Defensive testify as to the equanimity with which he viewed the general situation. The success of the enemy, which brought dismay to the Allied peoples in general and to many soldiers as well, seemed not to disturb him in the least. Perhaps it was because he knew that the breaking of the Allied line between Soissons and Reims was only an apparent success. Perhaps he felt relieved that the enemy had expended the substance of his gathered strength upon the achievement of a result so indecisive. At any rate, he displayed neither uneasiness over the progress of the enemy toward the Marne, nor any desire to arrest the hostile advance by throwing in his reserves across its path so long as that advance confined itself to the limits which have been described.

A mere defensive line, which might have been formed with his reserves, did not appeal to the strategic sense of Marshal Foch. He knew that the formation of such a line would be but an invitation to the German High Command to attempt to break it; and also that if committed to a mere lineal defence the striking power of his mass of manoeuvre would be lost. Unwilling to rob the mass of its potential velocity through its virtual immobilization in line, he held it intact pending the development of an opportunity for an offensive defence through counter-attack. He allowed the fifteen hostile divisions involved in the advance of the enemy to expend themselves upon his own broken divisions, and as the latter fell back, contented himself with placing fresh reserves in their rear, ready to take in flank any exploitation attempted by the enemy.

The untrained critic of these events points to the map and inquires for the trenches and the wire which eventually were to arrest the progress of the victorious German Army. He does not perceive in the masses of manoeuvre on the flanks a more effective bar than any fixed line of resistance. Or again, he describes the conditions which undoubtedly prevailed in the immediate front of the advancing enemy and declares unhesitatingly and with truth that the French line north of Château Thierry was completely broken, and that organised resistance had ceased in that quarter. From these facts he erroneously concludes that the road to Paris was open during the several days after the enemy crossed the Ourcq. Blinded by the smoke and confusion which exist on the tactical stage, or along the line of actual combat with the enemy, he is unable to see the broader setting of the strategical theatre. He neither considers the circumstances which obtained behind the German line, nor those behind the disintegrated forward line of the Allies.

And so he assumes that because a part of the forward battle line had disintegrated into minor units, some fugitive and all routed, no further resistance to the exhausted enemy was contemplated or possible. It apparently never occurs to him that fifteen divisions with a base of fifty kilometres could not proceed indefinitely, without relief, and eventually arrive at Paris, distant nearly a hundred miles from the starting point. Nor does it occur to him that the base of manoeuvre in any way limited the number of troops that could be supplied, or the distance which those troops that could be supplied might advance.

All these factors in the German problem Marshal Foch, however, understood so well that when the pressure of the enemy grew less toward the east, enabling the line to stabilise in that quarter between Reims and Château Thierry, and continued toward the west, he was able to divine accurately the intentions of the German High Command. The mass of his own reserves he had kept intact. When the shift westward of the German columns commenced, he possessed, besides the ten divisions with which he still opposed the fifteen German divisions in the salient, no less than thirteen French divisions in close reserve behind them, no slight obstacle on the road to Paris.

Even before the German columns reached the Ourcq, and before the decision to swing westward became evident, he had determined to stabilize the line of battle along the Marne between Château Thierry and Dormans and thence to Reims, and for this purpose had moved French troops up from the rear. He knew that a large force would not be necessary to check the enemy on this line, given the inevitable weakening in the driving power of the offensive, and that the slightest resistance would compel a halt for the purpose of relief and organisation. But the line northwest from Château Thierry possessed no such natural advantages as were offered by the Marne line. It constituted the real danger zone and might require the eventual use of the mass of manoeuvre.

The action of the 1st U. S. Division on May 28th at Cantigny had no doubt impressed Marshal Foch with the fact that other American troops were available for use. He now thought that they might be effectively employed in the organisation of the Marne line of resistance. Accordingly, on May 30th, the 2nd and 3rd U. S. Divisions were ordered forward for this purpose, to be distributed by small units among the French troops. They were in no sense summoned as divisions to fill an existing gap in the Allied line, for at the time they were called up the enemy was still being opposed along the Ourcq. But in their utilization at this juncture, Marshal Foch undoubtedly had a dual purpose. It enabled him to conserve in his mass of manoeuvre the more experienced French troops, and by the long-heralded appearance of the Americans to give encouragement to the French nation in an hour of great trial. It was politically an adroit move. As events turned out, it was also one which enabled whole American divisions soon to render military services beyond all expectations.

Out in front of the Marne line of defence and the mass of reserve divisions awaiting the next German move, a situation existed which was in itself desperate for those involved in it. Subordinate commanders, charged only with local responsibilities, and unapprised of the plans and intentions of the High Command, very naturally were alarmed by what they saw. The troops actually engaged in the conflict, and the people of the countryside, still less able to view the situation as a whole, only knew that a part of the Allied line had been routed, that the enemy was continuing to advance toward Paris, and that practically no reinforcements were being hurried forward to what seemed the critical point. Day by day the world at large followed on the map the progress of the Germans, and in dismay waited for the counter-attack which did not come. Such was the situation when the Americans reached the Marne.

4: The 3rd Division at Château Thierry

The 3rd U. S. Division, like the 1st, was a unit of the enlarged regular establishment. Assembled in one of the great southern training camps during the Fall of 1917, it was composed of old regimental organisations which had been divided and expanded so frequently that they had become regular regiments in name only. Some of the traditions, however, were retained by the regiments of the division, and it possessed a sprinkling of former regular officers even in the lower grades, as well as a small proportion of trained enlisted personnel. Arriving in France early in April, it was assigned to the Châteauvillain training area as part of the Third U. S. Corps, and after training there four or five weeks it was on the point of relieving the 26th U. S. Division in a quiet sector in the line when, on May 28th, preliminary notice of its transfer to the Marne was received. On May 30th, less artillery and engineers, it was placed at the disposition of General d'Esperey, commanding the Army Group of the North, who assigned it to the Sixth French Army.

The movement of the division commenced on the 30th when the 7th, or Divisional Machine Gun Battalion, proceeded with all haste overland for Condé-en-Brie. Outstripping the two infantry brigades which entrained that night for Montmirail, the machine gun battalion arrived at Château Thierry during the afternoon of the 31st, under urgent orders. There it was attached to the 10th Colonial Division, Thirty-Eighth French Corps, which was endeavouring to prevent the advance parties of the enemy from occupying the town. As the column formed by the two motorized companies of the battalion approached Château Thierry a great cloud of dust signalled its arrival. Before the head of the column reached the stone bridge spanning the Marne and leading into the town, the wild cheering of the throng of French soldiery through which it passed on the southern bank of the river gave further notice that the Americans were coming.

It was an inspiring moment. On the stone bridge stood the celebrated General Marchand of Fashoda fame, commanding the 10th Colonial Division, surrounded by a group of anxious staff officers. When through the dust, which obscured their identity for a time, he perceived that American troops were at last arriving he waved aloft his cap in greeting, followed by his staff, who vied with their commander in the enthusiasm of their welcome. Already the hostile artillery was firing upon Château Thierry. But a brief opportunity was afforded for reconnaissance before the American machine gunners, after twenty-four hours on the road, were posted in the northern outskirts of the town.

Château Thierry, with a normal population of about seven thousand inhabitants, lies closely nestled upon the slopes which ascend from the northern bank of the Marne to a plateau a hundred and fifty metres or more above the river. Once the home of La Fontaine, it is a picturesque town of stone buildings whose principal streets, each rising terrace-like above the other, parallel the stream. Below the edge of the plateau, an ancient *château*, with crenulated and bastioned walls,

CHÂTEAU THIERRY AND BELLEAU WOOD

rears itself above the trees and gardens which surround it. Along the main *boulevard* at the level of the river there stood, before the war, many lovely houses with walled gardens. Approaching from the east the Marne bends sharply south upon passing the town, as if to avoid a bare knoll known as Hill 204, which bars its direct course to the west. At no point more than seventy meters wide, but too deep to be forded, the stream meanders through a lovely valley walled in by two parallel ranges of hills. East of the town the crests of these lie about two kilometres apart, a narrow plain stretching along the base of the hills on the southern bank. South of the town the valley expands to a greater breadth.

Château Thierry is a railway junction of considerable importance in the Marne system of communications, and for this reason it was important to prevent the enemy from occupying the town. The distance to Paris by road is approximately eighty kilometres. Leaving the Marne at La Ferté-sous-Jouarre, twenty-six kilometres southwest of Château Thierry, an important national highway forms a chord to the bend which the river makes between those points, and passing to the north of Hill 204, crosses the stream at Château Thierry. Thence it follows the southern bank of the Marne to Épernay and Châlons. A main line of railway also follows the southern bank of the river, connecting Meaux, La Ferté-sous-Jouarre, Château Thierry, and Épernay. Branch lines connect Château Thierry with Soissons, about fifty kilometres to the north, and with Montmirail, about half that distance to the south.

During the night of the 31st, the enemy managed to bring more of his artillery to bear on the town, and bombarded it heavily with high explosive and gas shells. At dawn the position held by troops of the 10th Colonial Division and the American machine gun battalion along the edge of the plateau above the town was attacked by the enemy, who was temporarily repulsed.

Meantime the 9th Machine Gun Battalion of the 3rd Division had arrived at Montmirail by train late on the 31st, and marching rapidly to Château Thierry had taken up a position on the southern bank of the river, where it remained during the night. The Thirty-Eighth French Corps was established along the southern bank of the Marne between Dormans on the east and Château Thierry, with the 20th French Division on the right and the 10th Colonial Division on the left. On the 30th, the 3rd U. S. Division had been assigned a sector between Dormans and Domerey, the latter point being well downstream toward La Ferté-sous-Jouarre from Château Thierry. It was expected to assist, mingled with the French, in holding the crossings of the river along a front of nearly thirty kilometres.

On the night of the 31st, the Division Headquarters was established at Viels Maison, and the headquarters of the 5th and 6th Brigades at Crezancy and Ablois St. Martin, respectively. Each brigade was directed to post the battalions of one regiment in the front line, and one regiment in reserve. Over the former the French division commanders within the corps sector were given control, while the corps commander retained control of the regiments in reserve. As the troops arrived by train at Montmirail they were to be marched without delay to their posts in line and mingled by small units with the French commands.

Throughout the evening of June 1st, the 231st German Division continued to press toward Château Thierry, while farther to the north the main corps group, composed of the 10th Reserve, 33rd, and 237th Divisions, moved westward toward Hautevesnes, Bussières, and Belleau. The resistance at Château Thierry which its scouts and advance parties had developed during, the morning had not caused any delay in the progress of the main body toward the town. Small groups of French troops, continuing to resist here and there, had been rapidly brushed aside during the day, and nothing checked the movement southward of the enemy's main column till it was taken under the fire of a group of French artillery which General Degoutte, commanding the Twenty-first French Corps, had established near Château Thierry.

On the 2nd of June after being repulsed several times, the enemy gathered enough force to drive the French across the Marne. For a short while a number of the American machine gunners continued to resist, but were later compelled to abandon their positions, and gained the southern bank of the river with difficulty. Shortly after their passage of the stream, the stone bridge was blown up by order of General Marchand just as the enemy entered the town. Later, he made special mention of the conduct of the American machine gunners, who had hung on to their original posts to the last, and numbers of individual officers and men were decorated by him for their gallant conduct.

After occupying the portion of the town north of the river, the enemy made no serious attempt to cross the Marne in the face of the Thirty-Eighth French Corps. East of Château Thierry the villages of Brasles, Gland, Charteves, Jaulgonne, and others lying beyond toward Dormans along the base of the slopes on the north bank of the river,

THE NO MAN'S LAND

were quickly occupied 'as outposts by the Germans. Behind the crests of the towering range of hills overlooking these villages and the valley in their front the hostile artillery and larger enemy infantry groups were posted on the 3rd. West of Château Thierry, Hill 204, which commanded the town and the broader valley in its front, was also occupied on the night of the 2nd. The enemy pressure toward the west was now beginning to be felt. In that direction the 4th French Cavalry Division (dismounted) was guarding the crossings of the Marne toward La Ferté-sous-Jouarre, and later on the 2nd Battalion, 30th Infantry, was placed under its control and despatched to Saulchery-sur-Marne to meet the threat of the enemy from Hill 204.

5: West of Château Thierry; The 2nd Division

The 2nd U. S. Division had also been formed since the beginning of the war with expanded regiments of the old Regular Army and Marine Corps establishments. In point of personnel it was in no way different from the other so-called regular divisions save that the 4th Brigade was composed of the 5th and 6th Regiments of Marines, which retained a larger percentage of trained men than the infantry regiments of the Regular Army. In this respect these regiments possessed an undoubted asset. Arriving in France between June and October, 1917, as part of the original American Expeditionary Forces, the Marine and infantry regiments of the division were first concentrated in March, 1918, and on the 17th of that month, under the command of Major-General Omar Bundy, assigned to a quiet sector in the line east of Verdun for training in connection with French units. Twenty-four hours after entering the trenches the 23rd Infantry was unsuccessfully raided by the enemy. On the 23rd of March, the 2nd Field Artillery Brigade, which had arrived in France in January and which had undergone separate training at Valdahon, joined the division.

Early in May the brigade commanders took over the full control of their units from the French. On the 9th, in response to the call of Marshal Foch, the division was withdrawn from the trenches and entrained near Bar-le-Duc for Chaumont-en-Vexin near Beauvais in the Marne theatre of operations. There it was placed at the disposal of the Commanding General of the French Reserve Army Group, and on the 29th was ordered to move into the Beauvais front area, thus confirming the belief that it was to join the 1st U. S. Division, then in sector between Montdidier and Cantigny. Indeed, it is probable that the employment of the division in the prepared counter-attack of the

Allies, which we have already discussed, was originally contemplated. But when the enemy's third offensive of May 27th fully developed between Soissons and Reims, and the proposed counter-attack in the more western quarter was abandoned, the infantry of the division was ordered to move to the vicinity of Meaux. The division was now to be employed in meeting the hostile threat against Paris along the Marne.

Starting in trucks at 5 a.m. on the 31st, the infantry reached Meaux late that afternoon, while the artillery and transport followed by rail. At Trilport, the headquarters of the Sixth French Army, the division commander was informed that his command, when it took its place in the secondary line of defence, was to be broken up and distributed in the same manner as the 3rd U. S. Division. But General Bundy protested successfully against such a course of action and the division was ordered to be assembled intact at May-en-Multien, eighteen kilo-metres northeast of Meaux. From there the infantry, which alone had arrived, was directed at midnight to march to Montreuil-aux-Lions, about fifteen kilometres west of Château Thierry on the Paris road.

The night march of fifteen kilometres or more, after the fatigue of their preceding movements, entailed great hardships upon the troops, but they arrived at Montreuil-aux-Lions soon after daybreak on June 1st, while the artillery, after exhausting marches and counter-marches, had reached Cocherel, several miles to the west. Five kilometres be-yond Montreuil-aux-Lions near the village of Coupru the Paris road emerges from the woods upon a summit. Pressing up the western slope from Montreuil, the column was deployed left and right across the road at the forward edge of the Bois de Gros Jean, where it was halted and ordered to dig in. Then, it was known only that the enemy's columns were marching westward from Fère-en-Tardenois and the position selected was a most excellent one upon which to assemble the division in readiness.

While the troops were arriving and taking up their positions, Gen-eral Degoutte and a number of his staff officers, together with General Bundy and his chief of staff, held a conference beside the road near Coupru. General Degoutte favoured an immediate advance in order to counter-attack the enemy, but the Americans opposed the idea of throwing in the division without more assurance that the enemy's main column would be halted by an independent attack. They urged in preference that a line be established across the path of the advanc-ing enemy and that a definite defence be organised. The proposal was finally accepted, whereupon General Degoutte designated a position about six kilometres farther on as the one to be finally occupied. Again the division was set in motion, the 9th Infantry leading, and General Degoutte awaited the head of the column at the cross roads near the Paris farm two kilometres northwest of Coupru.

Upon being informed there by Colonel Upton, in response to his inquiry, how long the troops had been on the road, he remarked: "I don't suppose you will be able to do anything until you have had a rest?"

"Oh, yes," replied Colonel Upton, " the 9th Infantry can do anything you want done."

"Very well, then," replied General Degoutte, "take your regiment forward and deploy on the next ridge."

At this time the road was crowded with fugitive civilians. Small groups of French soldiers collected along the roadside to watch the Americans as they passed. The utmost despondency prevailed among the disorganised soldiery and civilians alike. Indeed, the more irresponsible ones were given over to a spirit of panic and loudly declared that the enemy would soon be in Paris, and that even now all was lost. As the troops pressed forward along the thronging road, irresponsible French officers and soldiers warned the Americans of the danger which they declared lay ahead. Others looked silently on as if the Americans were but courting certain destruction. But the 2nd Division was not dismayed. In the backwash of the battle line, when things have not gone well, the more timid may always be counted upon to portray the worst features of the situation at the front.

This they do, sometimes consciously, sometimes unconsciously, but always in order to justify or excuse their own presence in the rear. Nothing is more difficult than to gain an accurate knowledge of the actual condition of affairs from the fleeing inhabitants, the military stragglers, and the broken groups of soldiers that still cling together here and there as one passes forward through a retreating line. Experience, which the leaders at least of the 2nd Division possessed, teaches a soldier to discount the rumours of disaster that travel about the rear areas, and to seek for the facts along the battle line itself.

On the morning of June 1st, the facts on the immediate front of the division were bad enough. No definite line of resistance had yet been formed west of Château Thierry. The larger French units in front of Château Thierry had virtually dissolved into minor groups, and were being brushed aside like chaff by the enemy's columns, and

Château Thierry itself was being heavily bombarded. As the head of the division pressed on it saw a battery of howitzers in position near Coupru. Further along another battery was firing by the map, at high elevation with the trails of the guns dug in. A body of dismounted French cavalry was retiring along the Paris road. Upon seeing the Americans these turned back and took up a position south of the road in the Bois de la Marette facing east toward Hill 204.

But as events turned out the Germans never contemplated a direct advance along the Paris road from Château Thierry. Their scheme was much better,—to swing westwards, descending perpendicularly toward the main highway from the north. From Vaux to Montreuil-aux-Lions the Paris road, after leaving the Marne at Château Thierry and sweeping around the northern base of Hill 204, runs roughly west about twelve kilometres. Save for long descents to these villages it follows a ridge about two hundred kilometres above sea level. It was fortunate that the road lay just under or to the south of the crest of the ridge and could thus be used more freely for troop movements and purposes of supply. From the ridge, looking northeast and north in the direction from which the Germans were pressing, the hills descend toward a hollow which is marked by the line of road running northwest from Vaux through Bouresches, Belleau, Torcy, Bussières, and Gandelu. A line of narrow-gauge rail, branching from Château Thierry, also runs through these villages. Immediately northwest of Bouresches where the hills slope most sharply to the hollow, is the Bois de Belleau, and just north of the wood is the village of the same name.

Like most of the villages in this region, Belleau consisted of little more than a main street with a cross street, each about two hundred meters in length, with its church and houses built of stone, solidly, and with heavily walled enclosures. The cellars were well-constructed and afforded great defensive advantages. But its chief importance lay in the fact that it controlled all the cross roads leading to the Paris road from the north and northeast. The Germans would therefore have to pass west of Torcy to menace seriously the flank of the position selected by General Degoutte for the formation of a line of defence.

Upon reaching the Bois de Clérembauts, the 9th Infantry deployed with two battalions along the eastern edge north, and one battalion south of the road. Behind the 9th Infantry the 6th Marines turned off to the left and occupied the village of Lucy-le-Bocage, west of Bouresches, and south of the Bois de Belleau, while the 5th Marines occupied La Voie du Chatel and Marigny still further to the west.

Both regiments faced northward. The 23rd Infantry remained in the woods near Montreuil-aux-Lions. In this position, and covering an extraordinarily extended front of over nine kilometres, the division was formed before night on the 1st of June, with its right across the Paris road at a point about seven kilometres from Château Thierry.

But where was the enemy? Late in the evening General Degoutte notified General Bundy of an expected advance between Marigny and Gandelu from the north, and on the extreme left of the division. The 23rd Infantry, reinforced by one battalion of the 5th Marines, the 5th Machine Gun Battalion, and a company of Engineers, was aroused and sent to the quarter of supposed danger. But the alarm proved to be groundless. Indeed, throughout the day and night not a German was seen by the division. Even the advance parties of the enemy had not yet progressed so far west and south. Likewise, throughout the next day, the 2nd of June, while the enemy was forcing an entrance into Château Thierry and occupying Hill 204 and the northern bank of the Marne beyond the town, the. 2nd U. S. Division rested undisturbed.

On the morning of the 3rd, the divisional artillery was brought forward and posted. The 12th and 15th Regiments (75 mm. guns) were placed in support of the 4th and 3rd Brigades, respectively, while the 17th Regiment (155 mm. howitzers), reinforced by five groups of French artillery, remained at the disposal of the Artillery Brigade commander. The forward guns were posted in front of Isonge Farm and the woods between that point and La Pyramide. A train of thirty-two G.H.Q. trucks was impressed by the division staff and despatched forty-five kilometres for shell, making the round trip in thirteen hours over roads beset with many obstacles,—a fine piece of work on the part of the drivers and those in charge of the train. The French batteries remained well in the rear and continued to fire by the map. During the evening the 2nd Battalion of the 30th Infantry, 3rd U. S. Division, after a forced march *via* Saulchery, crossed the Marne and relieved the battalion of the 9th Infantry in support position at Mont-de-Bonneil, south of the Paris road. In that position it was able to meet the threat of the enemy from Hill 204.

On the 3rd, small parties of the enemy appeared on the hills to the north, and throughout the day trickled into the villages of Bouresches and Torcy, and into the Bois de Belleau, just beyond the American line. Though that line was a long, and necessarily weak one, an opportunity during the past two days and nights had been found to improve it somewhat. It was quite sufficient, as the event turned out, to arrest the progress of the exhausted enemy. Worn down by ceaseless fighting and marching, and without close contact with his main body, his advance parties were quite unable to assail the Americans. Indeed, compelled as they were to seek cover from the fire of the American batteries, they could only await the arrival of reinforcements and supplies. The Allies, on their part, were content to let them wait. No spectacular counter-attack was attempted.

The French in the Bois de la Marette were now placed under the control of the 3rd Brigade, and it was announced that during the night detachments of French troops would retire through the line, and that the position which had been organised by the division, and had hith-erto been a support position, would then become part of the front line. The command of the sector was to pass from the 164th French Division to the 2nd U. S. Division, with headquarters in Montreuil-aux-Lions, at 8 a.m. the following morning, June 4th. During the night the enemy displayed some activity in developing the Allied line on the left, north of Marigny, where hostile parties pressed forward against the 43rd French Division about 8 p.m. Several hours later they came in contact with the 23rd Infantry along the northern edge of Veuilly woods, but, having developed the American position, soon fell back.

June 3rd saw no spectacular combats between the Germans and the 2nd U. S. Division. Some results were, however, accomplished by the presence of the Americans. Not only did they successfully check the tired enemy, but they supplied a nucleus for the retreating groups of French soldiers on which to form, and converted to a useful purpose many small bodies which would otherwise have been ineffective. Best of all, their presence served to re-establish the morale of the French troops, who without any reinforcement had been retreating all the way from the Chemin des Dames. The discovery of a well-organised position, manned by fresh and vigorous troops of a new army, quickly dispelled the spirit of panic. In his report to the Sixth Army Com-mand, General Degoutte himself, much impressed with the spirit of the Americans, spoke of their "cheerful enthusiasm."

6: THE CONFERENCE OF JUNE 2ND

On the 2nd of June an important event occurred which clearly shows what view of the general situation Marshal Foch entertained at the time. At the very hour when to the world at large, and even to the Allied troops on the Marne, the threat of the enemy against Paris seemed the most grave, he appeared before the supreme, War Council at Versailles and did not even mention the supposed danger.

That the situation appeared satisfactory to him need not surprise us now. Commencing the operation with fifteen divisions, the enemy had increased his force in the salient between Soissons and Reims till it numbered twenty divisions. Opposed to these the Allies possessed twenty-two divisions in the front line and in support, including the 2nd and 3rd U. S. Divisions. Behind the support line, sixteen French divisions remained, in reserve. The 2nd Colonial Corps, which had been posted on June 1st across the Paris road at La Ferté-sous-Jouarre, was moving on the 2nd to Betz, where it was to remain on the 3rd. Furthermore, the line of defence on the Marne had been formed, and the mass of manoeuvre on the flank of the enemy's route to Paris concentrated, smoothly and without hindrance from the enemy, who was himself operating under great difficulties in the salient he had created.

It was with his thoughts turned to the future that Marshal Foch addressed the War Council. In attendance, among others, were Messrs. Lloyd George and Clemenceau, Lord Milner, Sir Douglas Haig, and General Pershing. To them, having for the learned of the possible reduction in the number of British combat divisions in France, the French leader represented in unmistakable language the necessity of maintaining the existing organisation of the British Army. Though it did not involve an actual reduction in numerical strength, he vigorously opposed the change, clearly foreseeing that if the existing number of combat divisions were maintained, the chances were much greater of eventually reconstituting the depleted strength of the army.

He then took up the subject of the comparative strength of the Allies and the enemy, and again directed the point of his discussion to a future need. What support in the way of manpower could he expect in the future? By studiously repeating apparently hasty and inaccurate underestimates of the Allied numbers, which called forth continual corrections from the members of the Council, he appears to have played admirably upon the fears of his audience and to have drawn out into the light of discussion the real intentions of their respective governments.

The British and French High Commands had recently experienced a forceful disillusion concerning their design to absorb the American troops within their own combat organisations. Despite the attitude of General Pershing, they had continued to hope for its success throughout the Spring of 1918. On May 2nd, under the pressure of events, the British Government had definitely undertaken to transport to France as many American troops as the available shipping would allow. In order to enable the secondary lines to be securely manned, pending the organisation of fresh British forces, it was agreed that ten American divisions were to receive their training and be equipped on the British front. A chance was thus opened for the actual if not the theoretical "brigading" with British troops. But it was thoroughly understood at the time the agreement was made that the American divisions should remain under the control of the American Command, and that their presence on the British front was to be but temporary. Under this understanding it came about that while some of these divisions were still arriving, no less than five were called to other quarters in order to enable American reinforcements to be assembled on the Marne. By June 2nd the eventual existence of a separate American army had become a practical certainty, while the use of Americans as Allied replacements was no longer a possibility.

This recent experience, together with the desire of Marshal Foch to obtain some idea of what support he might expect in the future, led the Conference to engage in an interesting and curious discussion, largely centring upon the American and British manpower problems. The result was that the needs of the immediate future were forcefully represented to the Government of the United States, while Lloyd George undertook on the part of Great Britain to reconsider the proposal to cut down the number of British divisions in France. Marshal Foch, on his part, turned again to the grave responsibility which had become his with a clearer understanding of what he might expect. It is possible that he had in mind even then the employment of the four British divisions which he was soon to call upon Sir Douglas Haig to furnish—the exact number of combat units by which it had been proposed to reduce the British Expeditionary Force.

7: The First Attack on Belleau Wood

On the night of the 4th of June the 23rd Infantry was relieved by French troops and moved into line between the 9th Infantry and the 6th Marines, thus reuniting the brigades, and shortening and strengthening the division front. Small German patrols had shown some activity on the 4th, but throughout that day and the day following the enemy displayed no intention of attacking. During the night of the 5th, a battalion of the 9th Infantry, relieving the French cavalry in the

55

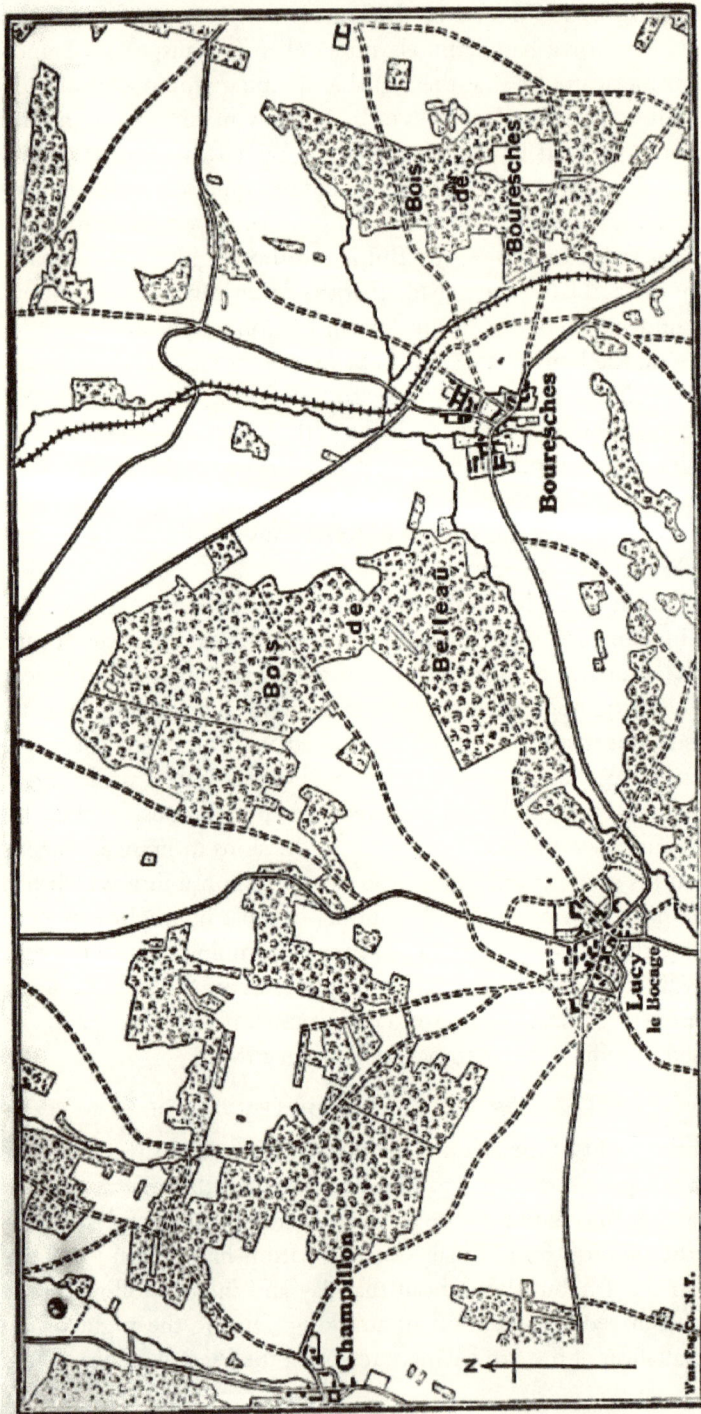

BELLEAU WOOD

Bois de la Marette, came under heavy yperite[1] shell fire from the direction of Hill 204 and the village of Vaux. But there was no real cause for alarm from that quarter. It was not believed that the Germans were capable of making a serious attack. Moreover, the situation to the east, along the river beyond Château Thierry, had become practically stabilized. There, as we have seen, an effective line of defence had been established along the southern bank of the river by the Thirty-Eighth French Corps, which now, connecting on its left with the 2nd U. S. Division, completely barred the crossings of the Marne.

It was, however, soon perceived that the villages of Bouresches and Belleau, and the Bois de Belleau, might be of considerable value to the enemy in future operations, and that it was desirable to improve the position of the line on the left of the Americans. The corps, therefore, planned an operation for the 6th of June which should accomplish these results.

That portion of the American line facing north extended from the Triangle brickworks on the right, due south of Bouresches, to Triangle 182, northwest of Lucy-le-Bocage, and thence to the woods north of Point 142 and south of Torcy. About opposite the centre of this line and between it and the village of Belleau, three kilometres to the north, lay the Bois de Belleau.

A view of the map does not reveal the real importance of this now famous position. Irregular in outline and nowhere more than a kilometre in breadth or depth, it consisted of a dense thicket which covered a rugged mass of rock rising sharply from the surrounding fields. A wild tangle of underbrush, and huge boulders strewn about as if in anger by a Titan hand, made of it a forbidding and all but impenetrable natural stronghold. Even after the fighting, during which the troops and innumerable shell cleared away much of the underbrush, it was extremely difficult to make one's way on foot through the place. Broken by one very deep steep ravine, and innumerable gullies, it afforded endless positions for small groups of riflemen and machine gunners, and in this respect was an economical as well as effective point to hold. Once the Americans held it they could compel the Germans to commence an eventual attack upon the Paris road from points as far north as Bussières and Gandelu.

On the other hand, for the Germans, its possession was essential since it afforded not only cover to the Château Thierry-Soissons road, but also a direct route to the Paris road behind a screen of rocky

---

1. Commonly known as "mustard" gas.

thicket, and a pivot of manoeuvre for a movement southward through Gandelu, which always remained a most serious threat to the Allies.

Early in the morning of the 6th of June, the 43rd French Division pushed northward from Marigny and established itself in position along the hills and in the wood, near Bussières, developing the growing strength of the enemy and the presence of a largely increased number of hostile guns. On the right of the French, the 1st and 3rd Battalions, 5th Marines, moved forward at 5 p.m. along the general line Champillon-Torcy, and reached their objectives at a distance of nearly fifteen hundred meters within two hours, capturing sixty-five prisoners. To the 6th Marines, Colonel Catlin commanding, had been assigned the task of taking Bouresches and Bois de Belleau. They were also to attack at 5 p.m., with two battalions. One of these was to move against the southern part of the wood and Bouresches, while the other was to emerge from the woods north of Lucy-le-Bocage and advance from the west upon the northern portion of the Bois de Belleau. The two attacks were to be concentric, and were expected to establish a line facing east at the far edge of the woods. But the American staff at this time lacked the experience to coordinate the action of the infantry and artillery, so that the Marines went forward without artillery preparation or adequate covering fire.

The battalion attacking the southern part of the Bois de Belleau and the village of Bouresches attained these objectives without much difficulty. The battalion which attacked the northern part of the Bois de Belleau went through the woods, and, according to the reports received at the time, emerged on the eastern edge, at some points gaining the road from the village of Belleau to Bouresches, which constituted its objective. But in the course of the attack, the regimental commander, who alone seems to have had the local situation well in hand, was wounded. The troops became confused in the dense woods, and great disorder prevailed among them, especially in the left battalion. Liaison between the units, large and small, failed utterly, and small groups moved here and there, counter-wise, and independent of each other. No adequate provision had been made for clearing the wood as the attack progressed, so that when the small forward groups successively emerged from the north-eastern corner of the thicket—and pressed on to the objective—the Belleau-Bouresches road—they came under the fire of hostile machine guns that remained on their flanks and further south in the Bois de Belleau.

The result was inevitable. Many of the company and platoon leaders and non-commissioned officers had become casualties. Those who remained knew little of the general scheme of the attack, and were quite unable to reorganise their disintegrated units and carry them forward. Dissolution set in, and with it a retrograde movement of the isolated groups commenced. One by one they trickled back to the starting point, suffering severe losses as they retired, without any orders or competent authority having apparently been given for the withdrawal. Nor does it appear that the enemy exerted any particular pressure. Simply confused and lacking in the necessary leadership, the men abandoned the whole northern part of the wood, and the men of the right battalion who had penetrated into the southern part, discovering during the night that their flank was exposed, likewise withdrew, though they did retain possession of a deep trench along the southern edge.

Better success, however, attended the attack on the extreme right. Here Bouresches was captured, with slight loss. The enemy was not present in strength, and the men went forward in fairly good order. But, having seized the village, the troops found it a very difficult place to hold. Cultivated fields closed in upon the gardens, and afforded excellent cover for small parties of the enemy. The streets of the village and all the approaches thereto were held under the fire of innumerable machine guns on Hill 201 and Hill 190, so that movement within the village proved to be impossible by day. The outposts were closely confined to the houses, and even into these the enemy's patrols managed at times to throw hand grenades. Snipers also were active. Near the railroad station, which was still held by the enemy, the Germans placed three trench mortars, operating them most actively. Nor was the friendly artillery able to render assistance, lacking knowledge, as it did, of the exact location of the troops. A trench mortar battery which made an attempt at support attracted heavy fire from the hostile artillery, causing the infantry to insist that the mortars suspend their activity. But, though lacking water, and ceaselessly harassed, the men clung to their captured village without thought of abandoning it.

The 23rd Infantry also encountered serious difficulties. Holding a line extending from the Paris road through the Triangle Farm to Hill 182 (Triangle) and then northward, it was expected to attack on the right of the Marines. The two together were to establish a line, virtually straight, from 211 through 182 to include the town of Bouresches, the 23rd Infantry serving as the pivot during the wheel to the right by the Marines and eventually conforming its advance to that of the lat-

All that can be seen of the Front Line trenches during the enemy bombardment

ter. At best the operation was an intricate one—too difficult in view of the inexperience of the minor leaders. The partially successful attack of the 6th Marines had been so planned that one battalion delivered a frontal attack from the west against the northern portion of Belleau Wood in an attempt to reach the Belleau-Bouresches road, while a second, swinging through the southern portion of the wood, sought to envelop the village of Bouresches from the south.

Without giving the 23rd Infantry any information as to his orders and plans, the officer directing the attack of the Marines undertook to pass part of the battalion that was to make the enveloping movement through the left of the line held by the 23rd Infantry, with the intention of effecting a wheel to the north when his own men were clear of those on his right. Ordered to conform to the movements of the Marines, however, and seeing them pass through their line, the officers on the left of the 23rd Infantry assumed that they had been misinformed as to their role, and instead of standing fast they led their units forward, across the railroad track, and into the wood east of Bouresches in a vain endeavour to follow and connect with the Marines.

It is not clear whether one or two companies of the 23rd Infantry engaged in this movement, and not at all clear where they went or what they did. Some of the men drifted back during the night; others returned the following day. There were many regrettable and unnecessary casualties among those who were thus misled, which gave rise to alarming reports at Division Headquarters to the effect that the 23rd Infantry had met with disaster. For a time it was believed that the enemy had assaulted in force and broken through the line held by the regiment, and the reserves were called upon. Indeed, no one knew during that night where the front line was located, for there was virtually no connection between the attacking units, and liaison from front to rear did not exist. Practically nothing was known of the position and strength of the enemy. The situation was exactly that which one familiar with the operations of inexperienced troops and an inexperienced staff might expect under the circumstances.

8: Hill 204

Daybreak of the 7th or June found the Americans busily engaged in strengthening Bouresches. Thence their line ran almost due west to Hill 181, continuing in the same general direction along the slopes above Torcy and Bussières. The Germans still held the railroad station in Bouresches and the northern outlet of the village. They likewise continued to occupy all but the southwest corner of the Bois de Belleau. But it was impossible for either side to accept the situation as it stood, since to each the possession of the Bois de Belleau appeared a necessity. During the night of June 7th-8th hostile patrols felt out the American position all along the line between Bouresches and Vaux, and a captured message disclosed the intention of the Germans to make an effort to recover Bouresches fully. Reinforcements of men and machine guns were, therefore, put into the village just before the German attempt was made and the hostile patrols were driven off without difficulty.

Meanwhile the Germans remained inactive in the region of Hill 204. Indeed, they had not yet brought up a sufficient force with which to launch a serious attack upon the American position, however weakly it was held. It is doubtful if they were yet apprised as to the exact nature of the force in their front. At any rate, when the real situation disclosed itself to the French Command, the advantage was perceived of occupying Hill 204 before the enemy should arrive in force sufficient to consolidate it.. Accordingly it was at first designed that the French Corps on the right of the 2nd Division should undertake the capture of the hill and that the Americans should cooperate in the attack by occupying the village of Vaux. This meant, however, a postponement of the attempt to clear the enemy out of Belleau Wood. Such a postponement the Americans did not desire, nor think wise, and their insistent representations caused the French to modify their plans. The 2nd Division was finally called on to advance only to a point midway between Monneaux and Vaux, for the purpose of establishing a straight line from Bourbelin across the middle of Hill 204.

Apart from the wood on its summit, Hill 204 was quite bare. Very steep, and open to view, it possessed little value as a position for artillery, but afforded excellent observation over the entire surrounding country, and in this respect would be invaluable to either side. American patrols had discovered the enemy in Vaux, and the hill itself was known to be occupied. To the 10th Colonial Division, which had come in on the right of the 2nd Division, the task of carrying the hill was assigned.

On the nights of June 7th, 8th, and 9th the line of the 9th U. S. Infantry was extended, and the French group in the Bois de la Marette, pivoting on the right of the 9th Infantry, advanced a little way up the southern slopes of the hill. This move was supported further to the right by three companies of the 30th Infantry, of the 3rd U. S. Division, which advanced at 10 p.m. Here, too, there was a grave lack of liaison between the attacking units. The hour for starting the attack was twice changed, and the usual confusion resulted. The Americans came under the fire of the French artillery and suffered serious casualties from it, as well as from the hostile guns. By 8:30 a.m. on the 10th, however, the 30th Infantry in the woods near the summit had established connection with the 9th Infantry on the slope west of Monneaux.

On the left the Marines were inactive. They still held a part of Bouresches and the south-western corner of Belleau Wood, but had made no further progress. Indeed, it was apparent to all that the enemy was at last forming, if not an aggressive, at least a definite line opposite the Americans. On the 9th his artillery had located Division Headquarters at Montreuil-aux-Lions and compelled it to retire several thousand yards to Bézu-le-Guéry, and movement within the sector became increasingly difficult. The actual number of casualties, however, was not excessive, only eleven hundred being sustained during the week. This small total includes all the minor cases as well as the permanent losses, and occurring as it did among green troops, is all the more clearly indicative of the slight nature of the opposition encountered up to this time. It should perhaps be added that the shrinkage resulting from the casualties was virtually made good by the arrival of nine hundred'and twenty-five replacements on the 8th.

9: The Second Attack on Belleau Wood

On June 9th it was finally decided to make another attempt to clear up the situation in the Bois de Belleau, and the Marine Brigade was designated to execute the task. The brigade commander, General Harbord, submitted a very definite and comprehensive plan for the complete capture of the position, but the Allied policy did not favour taking risks at this time, and the division commander was constrained to limit the operation. Accordingly only an attempt to seize the southern half of the wood was approved.

In thus restraining the ardour of the Americans, the French Command showed itself wisely cautious. It was not only confronted with the very difficult task of re-establishing a line of resistance along the faces of the salient which the enemy had driven into its territory, but it was limited in its operations by the delicate political situation in France. Its problem was therefore both military and political. Enormous movements of men and material had to be effected, and these demanded time. A false move of the reserves would be fatal; so that

American troops on the battlefield (Ville-en-Tardenois)

the most complete coordination of plans was necessary. Until the general situation became clearer and more definite, large local enterprises, however promising they might appear, could not be sanctioned. Furthermore, the French knew of the order of the German High Command that on no account were the Americans to be permitted to meet with a success. Therefore, if the maximum psychological effect of the entrance of these fresh, keen troops into the war was to be obtained, it was essential that they should be exploited with care. The use of American troops at this critical hour, pitifully few as they were, was a trump card which was not to be recklessly played. The proper play was to save them from a reverse, and in every way possible to magnify their worth in the eyes of the enemy.

This piece of French policy was completely successful. Fighting only winning battles, though small ones, the Americans were universally lauded. Justly entitled to high praise, their fighting powers were the subject of the wildest and most exaggerated reports which passed current everywhere. The French public, believing what it deeply desired to believe, drew from these reports untold comfort. The German public, in so far as the reports reached them—and the Allies took care of that—was alarmed by them. The American public to a large extent believes them still. Astutely coupled as they were with the carefully widespread news of a million Americans landed in France, their effect in June, 1918, defies our power of appreciation.

The task of clearing out the whole of Belleau Wood was a very minor one as military operations go, but it was none the less extremely difficult. Although the wood was small in area, it was, as we have seen, a very difficult piece of ground, and particularly favourable to the infiltration tactics of the Germans. There was also a ravine in it which the Marines called the "Death Ravine." Here the brush was so thick that men could pass unnoticed within a few feet of each other. Through this ravine, and another at the northwest corner of the wood, the Germans constantly filtered back into positions from which they were supposed to have been driven, and at all times during the fighting in the wood it was almost impossible to tell what parts were held by friend and what by foe.

The division staff, however, was learning rapidly from experience. In the first attack there had been no coordination between the artillery and the infantry, and although the large number of French and American guns had been ceaselessly active, yet they had not covered the advance itself. The attack for the 10th was more carefully prepared and coordinated. Assaulting at 5 a.m. after a splendid artillery preparation, the 1st Battalion, 6th Marines, advanced with a rush and reached its objective in twenty minutes, virtually without resistance. In fact, it was evident that the enemy did not hope to hold the southern portion of the wood and had abandoned it. Thus the line was advanced a distance of approximately five hundred yards.

A conference between the division and brigade commanders was held and a renewal of the attack ordered for the following morning. This time the entire wood was to be occupied. Though nothing definite was known about the northern part, it was assumed that the Germans would make no more serious attempt to hold it than they had done in the case of the southern part. As a matter of fact, they had firmly established themselves on the other side of the deep ravine, and when at 4:30 a.m. on the 11th the 2nd Battalion, 6th Marines, after another excellent artillery preparation and preceded by a rolling barrage, took up the advance, strong resistance was at once encountered. Progress ceased at the central ravine.

Along both edges of the wood small parties succeeded in working farther forward, and vague reports from these led to the idea at Brigade Headquarters that the success of the preceding day had been repeated, whereas the enemy's position remained virtually intact. The attack cost about two hundred casualties, though, on the other hand, about three hundred prisoners, thirty-five machine guns, and four trench mortars were captured. Again the troops had become hopelessly confused in the dense tangle of the wood. Little guidance was possible on the part of the officers, and the sketches and reports which they sent back were all but useless. Little real knowledge of the situation could be obtained at Division Headquarters, and the men in the fighting line simply drifted about more or less independently as before.

During the nights of June 11th and 12th, increasing efforts were made to carry out what was thought to be a cleaning-up of the wood when in reality the German defence had not been impaired in the least. The result was that little headway was made, and the Marine Brigade, which was rapidly reaching the point of exhaustion, was seen to be incapable of further effective efforts. The 3rd U. S. Division was called on for assistance, and between the 15th and the 23rd of June the 7th Infantry, with light casualties, acted as relief for the Marines.

Following upon the activities of the Americans on the 10th and 11th the Germans made several light counterattacks on Bouresches and the Bois de Belleau, Light but met with no particular success. They then undertook to drive the Americans out with intermittent bombardments in which mustard gas was so freely used that no serious attempt on their part was possible to push forward their infantry in force. During these bombardments the Americans held the edges of the wood lightly with machine guns, and withdrew the bulk of the defenders to Hill 181, which remained comparatively free of gas.

Though skirmishing and bombarding continued almost uninterruptedly day by day, it was not until the 23rd of June that the final task of cleaning up the wood was seriously undertaken. By that time the Staff had succeeded in fully informing itself, and the positions of the forward elements of the division were definitely located. During the 23rd and the next two days the wood was cleaned up with a minimum of loss to the infantry. In this work the artillery was most effective. Each one of six heavy batteries was given a definite area to search, firing at the rate of thirty rounds an hour. During the last hour the rate was raised to a hundred and twenty rounds, so that in all a total of twenty-eight hundred and eighty six-inch shells fell upon the few acres occupied by the enemy in the northern edge of the wood. Two and one-half tons of shell a minute soon made the stronghold untenable for the enemy. German officers, when captured, declared that those of their men who survived were simply bewildered by the fire of the American guns, and several of them begged to be shown the American "automatic six-inch howitzers" that proved their undoing.

The Bois de Belleau, which had given the Americans so much trouble, was finally taken through the coordinated efforts of the artillery and infantry with a total of not over two hundred and sixty casualties. More than three hundred prisoners, together with twenty-five machine guns, were taken, and a large number of German dead were counted in the captured woods. Then, as soon as the wood was entirely taken over and cleaned up, trenches were pushed out into the open in the direction of Torcy and Belleau, along which line slight progress was made in the course of the next few days.

10: VAUX

As soon as the Bois de Belleau was taken, the 2nd U. S. Division, with undiminished energy and enthusiasm, undertook to execute another task. For some time the French had been calling insistently for the capture of Vaux, and the Division Staff, which, with a month's experience behind it, was now functioning admirably, worked out the solution of the problem and completed its arrangements with a precision of detail that left nothing to be desired. Vaux lies in a hollow at the western base of Hill 204, its main street following the Paris-Metz road, which turns abruptly northward beyond the village to skirt the base of the hill. Its houses were strongly built and rather better than those of the average village of its size. Like the cellars of Bouresches, they were well prepared for defence, but this time no effort was to be made by the Americans to overrun machine guns with unsupported infantry. The Intelligence Section of the Division Staff managed to secure the most accurate information as to the garrison of the village, and with infinite care prepared a detailed plan of its defensive organisation. A concentration of artillery was then called for to render the defence innocuous before the infantry should reach the village. Also, owing to the fact that a distinct rise in the ground south of Vaux offered defilade to the flat trajectory of the American guns, a large number of howitzers were employed in the artillery preparation.

As the secrecy of the attack was not well kept, and the enemy took the precaution to readjust his defences and reinforce and rearrange his garrison, the thorough artillery preparation may be regarded as having saved the day. About dawn on the 1st of July it began, and was maintained for twelve consecutive hours at a rate of approximately five hundred rounds of high explosive shell per hour. The garrison was driven to the shelters and pinned under cover. Then two battalions of the 9th Infantry advanced in small groups, each with a carefully studied objective. Moving forward from the direction of Monneux and the western slope of Hill 204 on a front of two thousand yards, they were well covered from the enemy fire coming from the Bois de Bascon and the Bois des Pochets to the northeast of the village. Rushing upon the shelters when the artillery lifted, they overwhelmed the garrison and took nearly five hundred prisoners, twenty-five machine guns and six trench mortars, with a loss of but one officer and forty-five men killed; six officers and two hundred and eighty-four men gassed and wounded; and one officer and eleven men missing.

That night the Germans made a half-hearted attempt to launch a light counter-attack against the captured village, but it came to nothing. During the succeeding days they contented themselves with shelling the positions from which the Americans had driven them. Finally on July 4th the much needed relief of the weary 2nd Division by the 26th U. S. Division commenced, and by 8 a.m. July 10th was complete. The division then gradually withdrew to the secondary line

VAUX

about Montreuil-aux-Lions and Bézu-le-Guéry, where, on the 10th, it was visited by the American commander-in-chief, who bestowed the Distinguished Service Cross on thirty-four of its officers and men. It was recognised that the capture of Vaux was a most creditable small operation. The French Command and Staff had watched it with keen interest and were delighted with the result. Like Cantigny, it served to demonstrate what might be expected of the Americans when once they had become accustomed to the novel conditions of European warfare In less than a month the division had learned to act independently with every promise of efficiency.

11: Conclusion

The American position across the Paris road in early June, 1918, presented a front of nine thousand yards held by about twelve thousand rifles. Against it the Germans failed to develop any serious attack. Operating on the limited base of Soissons-Reims, they were faced with the necessity of crowding enough troops into the salient to hold its faces against French reserves, and to relieve already exhausted units, before they could hope to increase the pressure at the apex. Furthermore, inasmuch as only a certain number of troops can advance on a front of fixed width, a widening of the front at its southern extremity was necessary in order to make further progress possible in that quarter. Attempts to effect this widening by forcing back the French lines on the west of the salient and south, along the Marne, had been found as fruitless as they were feeble and had been abandoned altogether by the time the 2nd Division was encountered across the Paris road.

On the 3rd of June, when the 2nd Division was encountered by the enemy, there were on its front the equivalent of three divisions, two immediately opposed to it and two others whose sectors overlapped. One of the four was a first-class division; the others were third-class, and all were greatly reduced in numbers and much impaired in fighting power by exhaustion. On the 5th of June, another first-class division was squeezed in. Each of these divisions contained three infantry regiments and one field artillery regiment, and counted a rifle strength of about five thousand. The two first-class divisions had been in battle since May 27th, and the whole line was unsupported by heavy artillery, which the enemy had been quite unable to bring forward.

The fourth German offensive of 1918, which followed shortly, was essentially an attempt to widen the base of manoeuvre and, by breaking the Soissons re-entrant, provide a front of sufficient width for the continuation of the drive on Paris. It broke against the French Tenth Army under Mangin on the 9th of June, and was decisively defeated two days later. As early as the 10th, however, the enemy began to decrease his forces opposite the Americans west of Château Thierry, as if he already knew that the stubborn resistance of the Tenth Army was the death-knell of his Paris hopes. From this time on he maintained a distinctly defensive attitude. Several reliefs were effected, but, with a single exception, all the incoming divisions were of the third or fourth class, and the reduction in the number of divisions continued till on the 25th of June there were only two in line before the Americans, a bare minimum for defensive purposes.

The popular conception of the German Army advancing in full career upon Paris until abruptly halted by the sudden appearance of the 2nd Division at Château Thierry is utterly false. There is, in the first place, no evidence that the enemy made any serious attempt to cross the Marne at Château Thierry, contrary to the demands of his own strategical situation and in the face of French reserves. Neither was it at Château Thierry that the 2nd Division fought. There it was the machine gunners of .the 3rd Division who shared the honours with the French in making the enemy pay for the last piece of territory reached by his flood tide. West of Château Thierry the 2nd Division waited in selected positions for two days before the enemy's small advance parties appeared on the hills to the north, and in the local engagements which followed it was the Americans who invariably took the offensive against a line gradually strengthened (till June 10th) but as yet incapable of further serious effort. Their conduct in these engagements, during which they learned so much, was such as to merit the following General Order, which neither belittles nor overestimates their contribution to the saving of Paris and the turning of the tide.

The commander-in-chief desires to record in the General Orders of the American Expeditionary Forces his appreciation of the splendid courage, service, and sacrifice of the officers and. men of the First and Second Divisions of these Forces [2] during the recent operations in which these divisions participated and in which the enemy was checked by the resolute defence and counter-offensive of the Allied Armies.

---

2. It should be remembered here that the 3rd Division was at this time parcelled out among French units, and did not participate in the fighting "as a division."

These divisions, submitted fully for the first time to all the drastic tests of modern warfare, here themselves always with fine valour; their cooperation with their brothers-in-arms of the unified command was prompt and efficient and brought from their Allied comrades many expressions of sincere appreciation. The conduct of these brave men and that of their fallen comrades who made the supreme sacrifice has established a standard of service and prestige which every division of the American Expeditionary Forces will strive to emulate and preserve.

CHAPTER THREE

From the Marne to the Vesle

1: DEVELOPMENT OF THE AMERICAN FORCES

On March 28th, the day that General Foch was elevated to the supreme command, General Pershing tendered the available American troops in France to the Allied commander-in-chief without reservation as to their tactical employment. The offer was readily accepted and one American division—the 1st—was placed in the line in the Montdidier sector north of Paris. Then, when the third German offensive commenced, American reinforcements were called for in considerable numbers and hastily thrown into action under the tactical command of the French. The emergency which compelled their employment as reinforcements was so great as to extend beyond the time when the advance of the enemy was brought to a halt, and instead of being promptly withdrawn to the American sector north of Toul, a considerable number of American troops were kept on the Marne.

The organisation of a distinct American force in the Marne theatre was undertaken during the lull which followed the checking of the third German advance, broken only by local actions between June 13th and July 15th. American divisions were placed in line and on June 21st the headquarters of the First U. S. Corps, Major-General Hunter Liggett commanding, was established at La Ferté-sous-Jouarre. Under his command were grouped the 1st, 2nd, 4th, 26th, and 28th U. S. Divisions. During the following three weeks the corps operated under the Third French Corps, the headquarters of which was transferred from Chamigny to La Ferté. On July 4th, however, at midday, with his headquarters established in Château Lagny, General Liggett took over from the French the tactical command of the corps, to which was assigned the 167th French Division.

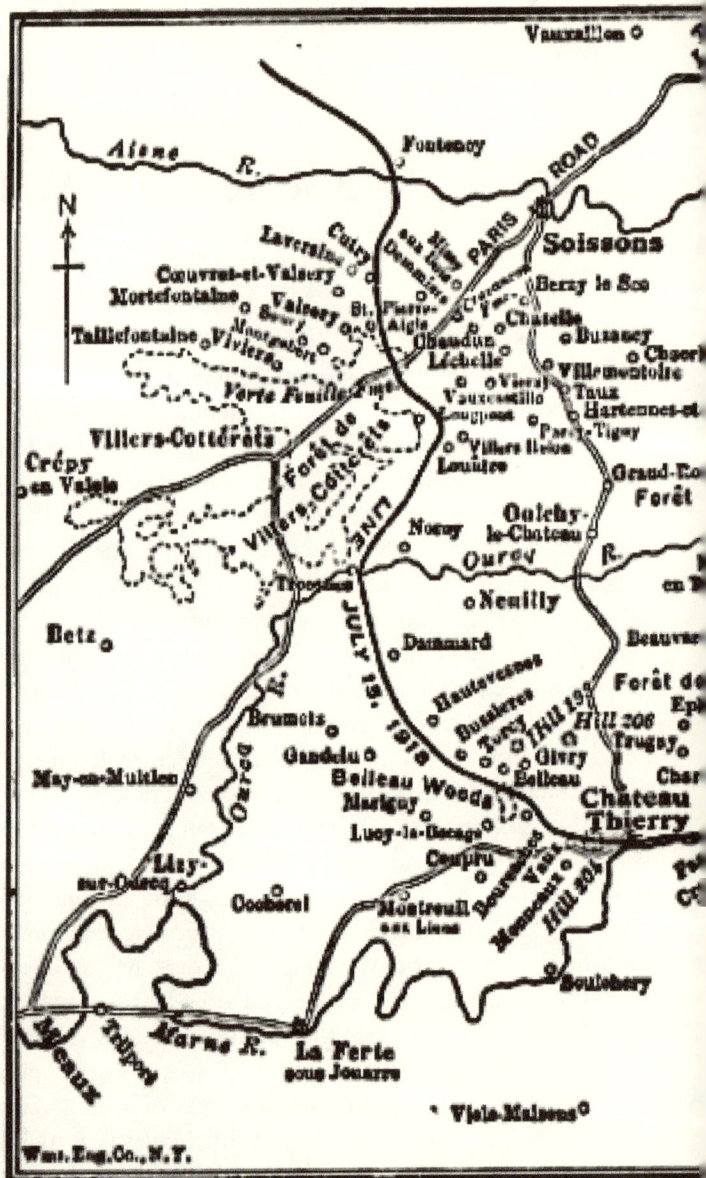

Vauxaillon

Aisne R.

Fontenoy

PARIS ROAD

N

Soissons

Laversine
Cutry
Montagne
Dommiers
Berzy le Sec

Couvres-et-Valsery
St. Pierre
Vaux
Chatelle
Bussacy

Mortefontaine
Valsery
Aigle
Chaudun
Charl

Taillefontaine
Vierzy
Villemontoire

Viviers
Montgobert
Léchelle
Taux

Verte Feuille Fme
Vierzy
Hartennes-et-

Vauxcastille
Longpont

Villers-Cotterêts
Paris Tigny

Forêt de
Villers Hel̃on
Louâtre

Crépy
en Valois

Forêt de

Oulchy-
le-Château

Grand-Roz
Forêt

Villers-Cotterêts
Noroy

Ourcq R.

LINE

en R

Troesnes
Neuilly

Betz

JULY 18, 1918
Dammard
Beauvar

Ourcq R.
Hautevesnes
Bussieres
Torcy
Hill 193
Forêt de
Eph

Brumets
Hill 206
Trugny

Gandelu
Givry
Char

May-en-Multien
Belleau Woods
Belleau

Marigny
Château
Thierry

Lucy-la-Bocage

Coupru
Vaux
Po
Cou

Lizy-
sur-Ourcq
Hill 205

Cocherel
Montreuil
Montrem
aux Lions

Meaux
Trilport
Ourcq R.
Soulohary

Marne R.
La Ferte
sous Jouarre

Viels-Maisons

Wm. Eng. Co., N.Y.

CHEMIN DES DAMES   Craonne

Aisne R.

Vesle R.   Basoches

Fismes

Bois   o Mont St.Martin
de Dole   Chéry
            o Chartreuve
            Dole
    o   o Dravegny   Reims
Mesles   Mesles
inges   o Coulonges
mols   o Chamery
        o Sergy
        o Clerges
        Courmont
        o Ronchères
    Fresnes
    Le-Charmel
    Forêt de Ris
                    Marne R.   15th 1918
Jaulgonne   Domecy
Mézy   Dormans
        LINE JULY
                        Ablois o   Épernay
Condé   Surmelin
en Brie
                    R.
                                    To Châlons

Montmirail

HE GERMAN ADVANCE

July 4th, 1918, is, therefore, an impressive day in the annals of the United States Army. It was most fitting that the National Anniversary should have witnessed what was in a sense the birth of the first distinctly American command in the great war, and that an American commander should have been placed on that day in command of French troops for the first time since the War of Independence.

Preparatory to the employment of the American divisions in two widely separated parts of the line, a new organisation was effected on July 14th. On that date Major-General Robert L. Bullard, formerly commanding the 1st U. S. Division, succeeded Major-General William M. Wright in command of the Third U. S. Corps, and established his headquarters in the Mortefontaine Château in Taillefontaine. To the Third U. S. Corps were now transferred the 1st and 2nd U. S. Divisions from the First U. S. Corps, while Major-General Charles P. Summerall succeeded to the command of the 1st U. S. Division. But while the administrative command of the Third U. S. Corps remained to General Bullard throughout the operations in which it was subsequently engaged while attached to the Tenth French Army, the divisions composing it fell under the tactical command of the Twentieth French Corps, under General Berdoulat.

So, too, of the four American divisions which at this time, with the 167th French Division, composed the First U. S. Corps, only the 26th Division remained under the tactical control of the corps commander. The 4th U. S. Division was divided between the Second and Seventh French Corps, and the 28th and 32nd U. S. Divisions were attached to the Thirty-Eighth French Corps.

Of the American divisions only the 1st, 2nd, 3rd, and 26th were at this time accompanied by their divisional artillery. To the First U. S. Corps was attached the 66th American Field Artillery Brigade, composed of the 146th and 148th Regiments with a total of forty-eight guns (155 mm. G.P.F.). To the Third U. S. Corps no American corps artillery units were attached, but to both corps were assigned French artillery units.

So much for the organisation of the American troops at the beginning of the Aisne-Marne Offensive. It is now necessary in order to understand the general situation at this time to review the events of the preceding weeks. The third German offensive of 1918, initiated May 27th, and concluded June 5th, succeeded in thrusting forward from the Aisne between Compiègne and Reims a great salient, the apex of which rested upon the Marne at Château Thierry. Extending from a point slightly west of Soissons along the Aisne, and then along the Vesle to Reims, the chord of this salient was approximately sixty-five kilometres in length, while from Fismes on the Vesle, midway between Soissons and Reims, the distance to Château Thierry was about thirty-five kilometres. The outline of the salient was roughly that of a figure jutting into the Allied line with three equal faces, each about forty-five kilometres in length. Its western face was intersected by the River Ourcq, which paralleled the Vesle midway between the Aisne and the Marne. On the Ourcq, at the centre of the figure, stood the town of Fère-en-Tardenois. From Soissons to Château Thierry a great highway paralleled the western face of the salient at a mean distance of about ten kilometres, while important railroad lines radiated from both of these towns and connected them.

The military situation resulting from the German successes of May was satisfactory neither to the Allies nor to the Germans. In the case of the Allies a dangerous re-entrant angle existed in their line, with the enemy within seventy kilometres of Paris. Upon the Germans, on the other hand, rested all the military disadvantages of occupying a deep and narrow salient position, while continued failure to improve the position would be deemed a confession of defeat. Military defeat at this juncture in the affairs of the Central Powers would carry with it the gravest political consequences. With the line finally stabilised along the Marne and with progress toward Paris definitely checked in the direction of Compiègne by Mangin's flank attack on June 11th, the problem remained how to exploit the successes which as yet had yielded no decisive results, however staggering to the Allies they may have been.

It was accordingly planned to press eastward for the purpose of developing the success already attained in that direction, with the capture of Reims as an immediate object and the roiling up of the French line towards Verdun and the Vosges as a more remote possibility. July 15th was appointed as the day for the resumption of the attack.

2: THE PLAN OF MARSHAL FOCH

There is support for the belief that even as early as the middle of June, Marshal Foch foresaw the development of the German plan and predicted a great success for the Allies, provided a sufficient mass of manoeuvre could be maintained at his disposal. Throughout the succeeding period of calm he appears to have been little perturbed by the impending storm. It is declared that when the enemy was finally halted

BATTLE OF THE MARNE

in his advance upon Paris, Marshal Foch exclaimed exultantly: "Enough of tactics! Enough of strategy! Let the victory come where it will!"—meaning, no doubt, that henceforth every Allied success should be fully exploited where it developed. It may be argued that this expression in itself disclosed a purely opportunist attitude of mind on his part, and that he had no settled plan at this time for assuming the offensive. The fact is, however, that no sooner had the advance of the enemy been definitely arrested along the general line Montdidier-Compiègne-Château Thierry-Reims by the Aisne Defensive (May 27th-June 5th) and the Montdidier-Noyon Defensive (June 9th-June 13th), than Marshal Foch began preparations for offensive action on a large scale.

We have seen that as soon as the German advance on the Somme had been brought to a halt on April 6th he had prepared a counter-attack to be delivered from the west in the region of Montdidier in the event the enemy should attempt a direct advance upon Paris from the north. Consequently a vast quantity of material and supplies had been collected in that quarter, and the French reserves had been so disposed as to be available for immediate employment. But the attack of the Germans on May 2 7th, having come east and not west of Compiègne, the contemplated counter-attack seemed at that time inadvisable, and was not attempted. Now again the marshal's thoughts turned to the possibility of counter-attacking from the west, this time in the event of the enemy resuming his advance upon Paris from the Marne. The preparations which had already been made might stand the Allies in good stead, and during the period of stabilisation between June 13th and July 15th they were continued expressly with a view to a counter-attack on a large scale in the neighbourhood of Soissons.

On June 13th, Marshal Foch wrote General Petain, commander-in-chief of the French armies, inviting his attention to the immense importance to the enemy of Soissons, and recommending that the roads and railways of which it formed the junction be kept under constant bombardment. It was only too obvious to him that Soissons was the heart of the whole system of supply within the Marne salient, of which the complex communication? radiating from Soissons were the arteries. Throughout the succeeding month, therefore, the Tenth French Army continued to feel out the enemy's positions on the west face of the salient between the Ourcq and the Aisne. Its commander. General Mangin, even manifested an impatient desire to undertake a serious operation in that quarter. Surveying the general situation from a higher viewpoint, however, Marshal Foch, with keen foresight, absolutely declined to sanction this.

The evidence is quite clear that prior to June 21st he had already in contemplation a great offensive action of his own. On that date a remarkable defensive policy was expressed in the orders of the French corps commanders of the Tenth and Sixth Armies. The line was to be held with a bare minimum of force, and the necessary troops were to be kept in the line as long as possible without relief, in order to permit the maximum conservation of reserves for use in contemplated offensive operations. Whether the plan under consideration at this time embodied a mere offensive defence, of great but still limited magnitude, or whether it contemplated a definite transition to a general offensive, the available evidence does not disclose. In spite of the impatience of General Mangin, it was not until the enemy's intentions had clearly revealed themselves that Marshal Foch committed himself to a definite plan of action. By July 10th, however, the hostile designs seemed to be well defined, and on the morning of the 14th he was certain as to the enemy's purpose. On that day he wrote: "The battle about to be engaged will comprise two phases, the first defensive, the second counteroffensive. The Fourth Army (east of Reims) must at all costs prevent the enemy from gaining ground."

In this decision the plan of Marshal Foch finally crystallized, and with it the orders of June 21st were significantly consistent. The plan does not, of course, establish more than a decision to deliver a counterattack, however extended, which must be distinguished from a transition to a general offensive.

So soon as the decision of Marshal Foch was taken, the four divisions constituting the Army of Paris were sent to the Fourth Army, General Gouraud commanding, east of Reims. Sufficient reinforcements were given also to the Sixth Army, General Degoutte commanding, between the Ourcq and Dormans, and to the Fifth Army, General Berthelot commanding, between the Sixth and Fourth Armies, to enable them to meet successfully the impending German attack east of Château Thierry. This done, instant measures were taken to effect the necessary concentration on the west face of the Marne salient, north of the Ourcq, for the execution of the second or counter-offensive phase of the battle, officially known in the American service as the Aisne-Marne Offensive.

3: The Champagne-Marne Defensive

On July 15th, the western and southern faces of the Marne salient were held by the German Seventh Army under von Boehn. With a front of approximately one hundred kilometres, its right rested near Tracy about fifteen kilometres east of Compiègne, while the left rested at a point slightly east of Jaulgonne, on the Marne, about fifteen kilometres east of Château Thierry. On its right lay the Eighteenth Army, under von Hutier, and on its left the First Army, under von Below.

Confronting the Seventh German Army, and overlapping both its flanks by about seven kilometres, were the Tenth French Army, under General Mangin, extending from the Compiègne-Noyon highway north of the Aisne to the Savières River, and the Sixth French Army, under General Degoutte, prolonging the line to the Marne at Château Thierry and beyond to the vicinity of Dormans. These two armies, together with the First and Third Armies, which held the line between the Somme and the Aisne, comprised the group of General Fayolle.

Unlike the preceding offensive, the time and place of the German attack of July 15th were fully foreseen. The very hour—midnight—at which the German artillery was to open was learned on the 14th. At 11:30 that night General Gouraud, commanding the Fourth French Army, east of Reims, commenced his counter-preparation. Nevertheless the Germans attacked along the entire front of his army, and of the Fifth Army between Reims and Dormans, extending their efforts to cross the Marne along the front of the Third and Thirty-Eighth Corps, east of Château Thierry on the right of the Sixth Army.

In meeting the enemy's attempt to cross the river, the 3rd U. S. Division alone of the six .American divisions on the Marne was heavily engaged. This division, though it had arrived in France as late as April, and had been hastily thrust into the line late in May without any experience, had acquitted itself with credit on the right of the 2nd U. S. Division at Château Thierry. Here it had helped to man the crossings of the Marne during the first week of June and had earned distinction particularly for its machine gunners. Now it was attached to the Thirty-Eighth French Corps, under General de Montdesir, and held the front line in the right sector of the corps, between the 39th and 125th French Divisions. Behind it, and the 125th was posted the infantry of the 28th U. S. Division, composed of units of the Pennsylvania National Guard, which had arrived in France even later than the 3rd Division, and at this time was wholly without experience of war.

The position assigned the 3rd Division was admirably adapted to the defence of the river crossings east of Château Thierry. Lying along the steep and heavily wooded hills which parallel the southern bank

XVIII
von Hutier

VII
von Boehn

I
F. von Below

X
Mangin

V
Berthelot

VI
Degoutte

Laon
EM XXVII CR

Soissons
Compiegne
Reims
Chateau
Thierry

18 End of June
1
26 End of June
3R End of June
51R
10 End of June
20 July 5
117 Beginning of July
26 July 4
239
113 June 19
103 July 7
50 July 11
200

July 2 2b 37 June 25
46R July 6
19E July 6
10R June 23
33 June 27
36 June 26

11B June 23
XXV R July 4
Fère en Tardenois

168
1US
40C
4US

2 & 6 DC

2US
4
18
73
3C
30C
20
77
100 IC
14
71 27
45
7 10
20

Aisne
Aisne
Veale
Marne R.
Marne R.
Vesle

Dormans
Jaulgonne
Staabs
14R
241

Opposing orders of battle, July 15. 1918

Wms. Eng. Co., N.Y.

of the Marne, it was a position of great natural advantages, though little opportunity had been found to strengthen it. Along the railroad line skirting the river, isolated strong points were indeed established, and farther back along the slopes of the hills the beginnings of a subsequently continuous line, known as the Aqueduct line, had been made. But from the time the sector was taken over by the division, work on the defences was rendered almost impossible by hostile fire, the constant shifting of units, and the lack of engineer personnel.

The attempt which the enemy made to cross on the front of the 3rd Division was no doubt suggested by the topography of the position as well as the weakness of the defensive works. On the right of its sector the line of hills was cleft by a deep valley running north and south, through which flowed a small stream—the Surmelin. The entrance to this valley was commanded by German guns north of the Marne, while the road ascending it offered an excellent approach by which the enemy might filter southward between the Thirty-Eighth and Third French Corps and thus turn the flanks of the Sixth and Fifth Armies. Possibly political reasons also contributed to the German desire to force a crossing on the front of the newly arrived American unit.

From left to right the position of the 3rd Division was held by the 4th, 7th, 30th, and 38th Infantry Regiments, with one battalion of each regiment in the front line, disposed in depth, and one platoon of each battalion on the river bank. The Aqueduct line was designated as the main line of resistance, and all forward posts were ordered to be held. Behind the ridge was stationed the artillery. The accepted French method of holding a position in strength on the counter-slope with slight forces forward of the crest was not employed, probably because it was unsuited to the holding of a river-crossing.

Opposite, the enemy had massed eighty-four batteries of various calibres. Well before dawn, after a night of abnormal calm, the hostile fire fell upon the American position, subjecting it to an intense bombardment with both high explosive and gas shells. The American artillery, which had succeeded in getting into position during the night, likewise opened an effective fire, anticipating the German bombardment by some minutes, and directing its attention to the river-crossings and the enemy's assembly places. Fully informed of the intentions of the Germans, the divisional artillery had carefully reconnoitred the hostile position and registered upon it, so that its fire, which was in the nature of a counter-preparation, seriously impeded the enemy's movements and inflicted heavy losses upon his troops. In spite of this, however, the crossing was attempted about 3:20 a.m.

No attempt to cross was made in front of the 4th Infantry on the left. Opposite the 7th Infantry the 395th German Regiment, issuing from the Bois de Barbillon, was brought under very accurate artillery fire. Badly cut up and demoralised, it probably succeeded in throwing but one company across the river. Small bodies of the enemy crossed the river in boats near La Ru Chailly Farm, and at other points; and at Mézy, under cover of smoke screens, two pontoon bridges were thrown, over which troops of the 10th and 36th German Divisions crossed in considerable numbers. Between these parties of the enemy and the advance groups in front of the American right wing a desperate hand-to-hand encounter ensued. The resistance which the enemy met with in this quarter seems to have been unexpected by him.

Though the 38th Infantry finally succeeded in hurling back the troops which had crossed over the more easterly of the two bridges, the Germans sought to advance from Mézy south and southwest against the 7th and 30th Infantry under cover of a rolling barrage. Their object was to penetrate between these two regiments, where confusion and disorder had reigned for a time. But before the attack was developed the position was reorganised, and a strong defensive line facing east with its left in front of the village of Fossoy and its right resting on the Bois d'Agremont confronted the enemy. Reaching this line the assaulting troops penetrated it with small groups at various points, but were unable to break it.

After failing to gain a hold on the southern bank of the river opposite the 38th Infantry, the enemy abandoned his efforts in that quarter in favour of a crossing near Varennes in the sector of the 125th French Division on the right of the 3rd, where, about 5 a.m., he met with a temporary success that exposed the right flank of the 38th Infantry. About 8 o'clock, after the attack from Mézy had been broken up, the 30th Infantry had withdrawn its right to a position along the Fossoy-Crezancy road without notifying the 38th Infantry. Exposure of both its flanks by the shift in position of the 30th Infantry on the left, and the retrograde movement of the French on its right, compelled the 38th Infantry to refuse its wings, thus forming a three-sided square with its centre remaining on the river bank. In this formation it succeeded in beating off a fresh attack upon its left delivered from Mézy about 10:30 a.m., and later in establishing its right on the hills east of the Surmelin until the regiment was withdrawn during the night to the so-called Aqueduct line. Repeated attempts by the Germans to break the line further west also ended in failure, and were definitely abandoned before the night of the 15th. The following day the enemy continued his efforts to penetrate between the 38th Infantry and the 125th French Division, but in vain.

On the 15th, however, he had forced a crossing on a wide front opposite the Third French Corps, which included the 125th French Division on the left, actively supported by elements of the 28th U. S. Division. This corps, with the Fifth Army on its right, had fallen back some distance. But by the night of the 16th small parties of the 3rd Division had reoccupied the posts along the river bank and the village of Mézy, and communication with the 125th French Division was re-established. Finally, on the 17th, the Thirty-Eighth French Corps and the Fifth French Army succeeded in forcing the enemy back all along their fronts, leaving him in possession of a small salient on the front of the Third French Corps. Such was the situation east of Château Thierry when the counter-offensive of the 18th was launched.

The battle of the 15th of July was engaged under exactly the conditions Marshal Foch desired. When the German Seventh and First Armies on the 15th forced a crossing of the Marne opposite the Sixth and Fifth French Armies, and seemed the following day to be pressing their success toward Epernay, with the resolution of true military genius he resisted all appeals to reinforce his right. Speaking of the enemy's successes in the east, General Fayolle said at this time: "That makes no difference. His progress there will soon cease," clearly expressing in these words the view of Marshal Foch.

General Fayolle's prediction proved to be accurate. Having advanced several kilometres southward on a wide front opposite the Fifth and the right of the Sixth French Armies, on the 17th the enemy was definitely checked, and the danger which had seemed so grave was over before the counter-offensive, or second phase of the battle, was undertaken on the 18th by Marshal Foch.

4: Preparing the Counter-Drive

As soon as Marshal Foch learned on the morning of the 15th that the enemy's attack east of Reims had been successfully resisted by the Fourth French Army, he disregarded with superb audacity the success gained by the Germans between Chateau Thierry and Reims and at once undertook the consummation of his counter-offensive.

Driving four hours in his motor to meet Marshal Haig, he apprised him for the first time of his scheme, and requested the transfer south of the Aisne of four British divisions. This request Marshal Haig promptly acceded to with characteristic loyalty, thus enabling the French commander to turn with full confidence to the execution of his plan.

Though verbal orders only were given to the Tenth and Sixth French Armies for the attack of the 18th, the various corps orders reveal clearly enough the ideas of Marshal Foch. They show that the specified objectives for the attack were very limited indeed. The attack was no doubt capable of development, but it appears to have been designed with the definite purpose of relieving the embarrassing situation in which the Allies had been placed by the advance of the Germans across the Aisne. Though Marshal Foch had undoubtedly had offensive operations in mind since the time of his elevation to the supreme command, and was now putting them into execution, he in no sense intended to initiate a general offensive on the part of the Allies unless through some weakness developed by the enemy he saw a chance to extend his initial drive into a more and more extensive general action. "Let the victory come where it will!" the marshal had exclaimed. He was striking for an opening and was ready to seize it when it appeared.

A tremendous blow was to be delivered to the Seventh German Army, now fully committed to an attack toward the east, by the Tenth French Army between the Aisne and the Ourcq. The object was to crush in the west face of the salient and cut the main lines of communication leading south from Soissons. The Sixth and Fifth French Armies were to exert sufficient pressure upon von Boehn's centre and left to hold them in place and prevent the reinforcement of his right. In the first stage of the operation, the Sixth Army was to fight a holding action while the Tenth Army made its thrust toward the east. In the event of the Tenth Army succeeding in breaking through the German line north of the Ourcq, a withdrawal by the enemy from the south would become impossible. Short of this result the Tenth Army, pivoting on the Aisne west of Soissons, and the Sixth Army, prolonging its line to the right, were to swing to the left and force the enemy across the Vesle, thus wiping out the salient, while the Fifth Army cooperated from the east by exerting pressure upon the eastern face of the salient. The taking of Soissons at this time was not contemplated.

The necessary concentration for the attack involved the very rapid movement of reserves. From the First French Army in the Amiens sector was drawn the 41st French Division; from the Third French

Army north of the Aisne, the 19th, 58th, and 72nd French Divisions; from the Sixth French Army the 2nd U. S. Division, which had been relieved in the line by the 26th on July 6th-8th; from rear areas the 1st and 5th French and the 1st U. S. Divisions; and from the British Front the 15th and 34th British Divisions. The Second Colonial Corps, composed of the 2nd, 4th, and 6th Colonial Divisions, was moved up from the defences of Paris. In a minimum of time there were placed in the front line and in support on the front of the Tenth Army, between the Aisne and the Ourcq, fifteen divisions, opposed to which there were but six inferior German divisions with four in close reserve.

At the disposal of the Sixth French Army there was a total of eighteen divisions, including four American divisions, with twelve divisions in the front line opposing an equal number of German units. Near Gonesse the 4th, and in the region of Crécy the 2nd and 6th French (dismounted) Cavalry Divisions were stationed. This juxtaposition of forces resulted from the concurrent prosecution of the German offensive initiated on the 15th, and the Allied concentration north of the Ourcq, and is graphically illustrated by the appended chart, which, when compared with the chart showing the order of battle of July 15th, discloses both the French and German movements during the period in which the Allies changed from the defensive to the offensive.

Von Boehn had drawn heavily on his reserves during the 15th, 16th, and 17th, but nine divisions remaining on the 18th in reserve in the Seventh Army north of the Ourcq. With his right wing, which confronted the Tenth French Army, virtually unaltered in position and in its constitution, his left flank had been extended eastward from Jaulgonne a distance of about twenty-five kilometres, taking over part of the front formerly held by von Below's First Army. This extension had been effected by throwing into the line no less than fourteen fresh divisions for the purpose of exploiting the temporary success of the 15th and 16th. Thus, from the beginning of his attack the whole weight of his influence trended toward the southeast, diagonally toward his left.

But, while von Boehn's movements trended southeast, those of Marshal Foch trended northwest in preparation for the blow he was to deliver. Schematically, these concurrent movements may be regarded as two sliding forces, gradually developing pressure along parallel lines in opposite directions. On the part of Marshal Foch it was a masterly manoeuvre, daringly and cleverly conceived and skilfully executed. It was worthy in every respect of his great reputation. In contemplating

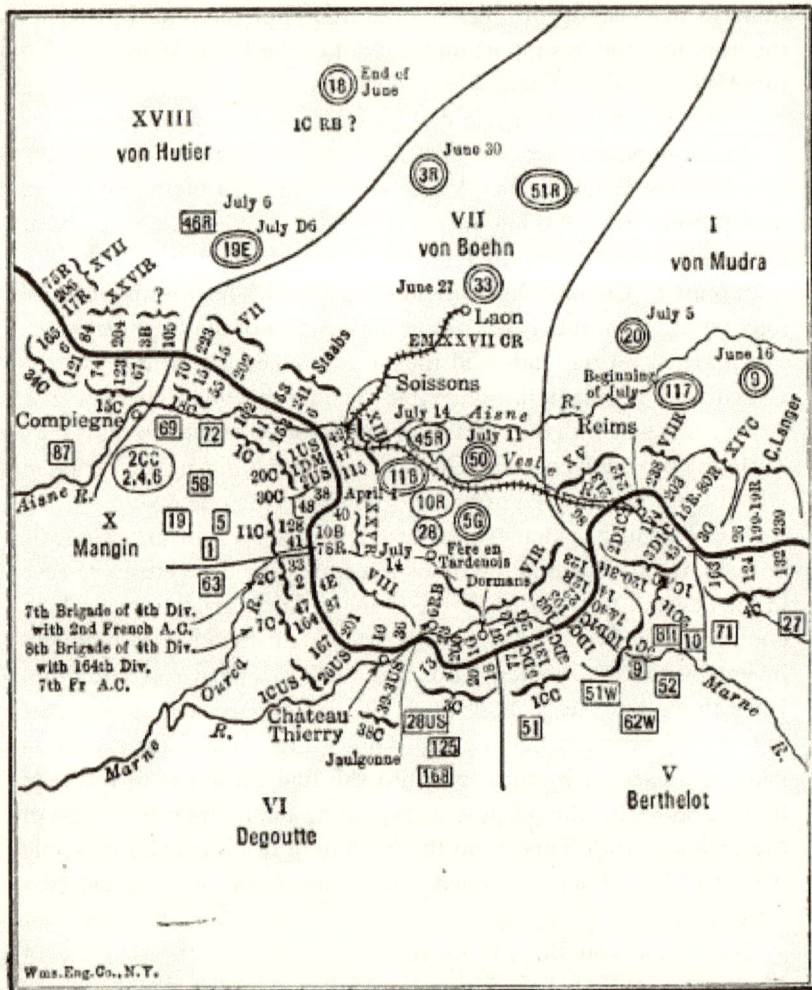

OPPOSING ORDERS OF BATTLE, JULY 18, 1918

it one marvels at the daring which enabled him to turn his back, in a sense, upon the most seriously threatened quarter of his line while preparing a counter-blow to be delivered at the point most distantly removed from that of his own gravest danger.

Never in the course of the war were the preparations for an operation on so large a scale conducted with more secrecy than were those for the counter-offensive of July 18th. The great bulk of the necessary supplies and material was transported by night, while every effort was made not to increase the apparent activity during the day, or to disclose during the latter stages of the preparation any marked increase of activity. North of the Ourcq, where the plan involved a concentration of force, the method adopted to conceal the movement was that of distributing the shock divisions in the rear areas, whence they were rushed forward into line at the eleventh hour. On July 17th, there were in the line of the Tenth Army but three of the nine divisions which were to attack on the morning of the 18th, and in close support not a single division that was later engaged. The Forêt de Retz, east of Villers-Cotterêts, was most skilfully utilized to the fullest possible extent to screen the concentration.

To add to the surprise of the attack, it was not heralded, in accordance with the tactical conceptions of 1916 and 1917, by a long period of destructive artillery fire during which the enemy might undertake the strengthening of rearward lines. The methods first employed by the enemy at Riga, and consistently in his offensives of 1918, were adopted, according to which camouflage, night movement, and the use of abandoned positions were fully resorted to for the concealment of the artillery concentration. Registration was obtained by the alternating fire of old and new batteries, without increasing the number of active guns, and by an increased volume of fire for the active guns extending over a long period which enabled more guns to register.

Under these conditions confusion and disorder were inevitable within the divisional units, which were taxed to the utmost by the often conflicting demands of speed and secrecy, of time and space. Units so small, however, were but pawns upon the far-flung board of the Allied High Command. Viewed in its entirety the game displays the most amazing and faultlessly adroit movements of the major pieces.

5: The Spear-Head of the Attack

The mission of the Tenth Army was to break the hostile line between the Aisne and the Ourcq and to push on without stopping in the direction of Fère-en-Tardenois. Its first objective was the ridge west of Pernant, Saconin-Breuil, Chaudun, Vierzy, and Villers-Helon, while its second objective lay along the plateau between Chacrise and Oulchy-le-Château. When the latter objective had been attained, further progress was to be ordered depending on the course of the battle.

On the morning of the 18th, the Tenth Army, composed of five corps and twenty-three divisions, was formed as shown on the chart. Six divisions were held in close support and six in reserve, including the 15th and 34th British Divisions. The attack was to be delivered by the First, Twentieth, Thirtieth, and Eleventh Corps, with a total of nine divisions in the front line, between the Aisne and the Ourcq, while the Eighteenth Corps north of the Aisne was to form the pivot on which the army was eventually to swing. The First Corps was to seize the plateau south of the Aisne from Pernant to Berzy-le-Sec inclusive, and to bring the outlets of Soissons under a heavy fire. With its axis passing through Trois Peupliers, Dommiers, Chaudun, and Ville-montoire, the Twentieth Corps was to encircle the Forêt de Retz from the north and south, seize Chaudun and Vierzy, and endeavour to reach the plateau northeast of Hartennes, from which position it was to hold the southern outlet from the Ravin de la Crise. On its right the Thirtieth Corps was to push across the Savières River and attack the front between Villers-Helon and Montremembœuf Farm, from which line it was to press on past the crest of St. Gervais-Bois d'Ercy in the direction of Fère-en-Tardenois, with the Eleventh Corps on its right conforming to its movements.

Attached to the Twentieth French Corps were the I St and 2nd American Divisions, composing the Third U. S. Corps, under General Bullard. They were undoubtedly the most highly trained and experienced units in the American Expeditionary Force. While they should not be regarded as regular divisions in the sense of regular troops prior to the war, it is true that many of the traditions of the old regimental organisations composing them did remain, and there was in these divisions a sprinkling of young field officers who had been subalterns in the regular service before the war. Their principal asset as fighting units lay in their comparatively long experience in France. Arriving in France in June and October, 191 7, respectively, the 1st and 2nd U. S. Divisions had not only had experience in the trenches during the winter following but had won deserved fame at Cantigny and near Château Thierry. They were now to constitute the spear-head of the

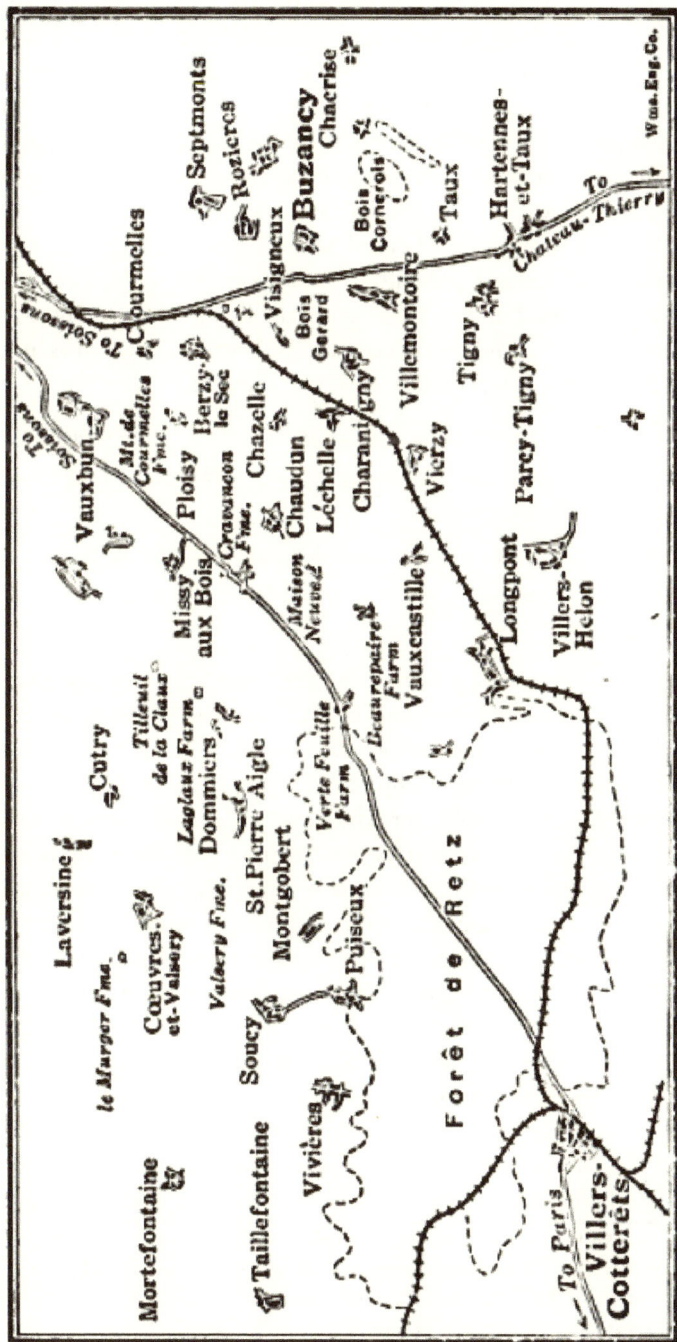

WHERE THE SPEAR-HEAD STRUCK

attack. Of all the infantry of the famous Twentieth Corps,[1] Americans were to comprise not less than four-fifths. No other commentary is necessary to establish the high estimate which Marshal Foch had formed of them. In no sense was their presence in the line at so critical a point accidental. They were brought there from distant points with a full and accurate knowledge of their proved capacity, and General Bullard was right in calling attention before the battle to the high distinction and honour thus conferred on his command.

The Germans were not far behind Marshal Foch in their estimate of the Americans. Immediately after the appearance of the 2nd Division near Château Thierry a German Intelligence document was captured in which the 2nd was declared to be "perhaps even an assault division." Again, it was reported in this document that:

The quality of the men must be characterized as 'remarkable.'

At the present time they require only proper training to make them formidable adversaries.

The spirit of the men is fresh and full of naive confidence.

The following statement by a prisoner is characteristic: 'We kill or we are killed!'

It must be remembered, however, that the losses among the original commissioned and enlisted personnel of these divisions had been abnormally heavy in May and June—especially among the former—and that experienced field officers were impossible of replacement. It must also be remembered that not only were the ranks of both divisions refilled with partially trained replacements, but that they had been subjected to a gruelling ordeal extending over many days of fighting and labour, marching and bivouacking in the open, without rest or relaxation from the strain of active operations. Neither of these divisions was, on July 18th, a fresh division in any sense of the word. While their achievements undoubtedly far exceeded all expectations, it is fortunate that they were not confronted by German troops of the first quality, or called upon to assail the same positions held in greater force.

The fact must not be ignored in estimating the success of the Twentieth Corps that on the 18th its infantry outnumbered the infantry of the Eighteenth German Corps opposed to it in the proportion

---

1. At the outbreak of the war, and during the battles of Morhange and the Grand Couronne, the Twentieth Corps was commanded by General F. Foch. Before the war, as commander of the Twentieth Corps, with headquarters at Nancy, the future marshal was regarded as holding the post of honour of the French Army.

of at least five to three, and that the artillery superiority on its side was no less marked. The best troops of the Seventh German Army had either been committed to the attack east of Château Thierry, or, having been employed in the previous offensive, were resting in reserve. No indication of the impending blow had caused von Boehn to reinforce the right of his line, so that the fifteen divisions of the Tenth French Army in the front line and in close support between the Aisne and the Ourcq were confronted by but six inferior German divisions in the front line, with four divisions in close reserve.

But there are other factors to be considered if we are to understand the American troops in this battle. Seemingly unessential aspects of events often affect the spirit and action of men to an extent out of all proportion to the importance subsequently attached to them. This is especially true as to soldiers. Indeed, the psychological influence of the smiling country about them, and of the weather conditions which prevailed during the operations on the Aisne and Marne in July, 1918, was no unimportant factor in the American success. Almost perfect were the days which succeeded the brilliant sunrise of the 18th. In complete harmony with the beauty of surrounding nature, the blue skies, the genial warmth, the balmy air of the sunny days and starlit nights, engraved upon the minds of men the one common impression which they retain of those tortured hours, an impression only more firmly fixed, by reason of the very contrast between the peace of nature and the discord of human strife.

At this time, too, the spirit of the Americans was wrought to such a temper that no thought of the possibility of failure entered into their minds. Leaders there may have been whose minds dwelt upon the holiness of their mission, and who transmitted something of the spirit of their devotion to those who followed, but one need not dwell upon the exalted motives of the soldiery, their patriotic fervour, and the like. The exaltation of the spirit that rested upon them was the determination to win in this hour when the supreme test was imposed upon American soldiers fighting side by side with their Allies—French, British, Moroccans, and Algerians. They were inspired by an almost fierce spirit of competition rather than by any conscious resolve to do or perish in a sacred cause—the desire to win and to "show what they were made of," rather than a vision of righteousness.

6: THE 1ST AND 2ND U. S. DIVISIONS BEFORE THE BATTLE

On July 8th and 9th, the 1st U. S. Division had been relieved from

SOME TYPES OF
AMERICAN SOLDIERS

the Montdidier sector north of the Aisne, where on May 28th it had brilliantly captured the position of Cantigny, and had been withdrawn from the line to a rest area north of Beauvais. There, with the exception of the 2nd Infantry Brigade and the 7th Field Artillery Brigade, which were grouped between Froissy and Breteuil in reserve of the Tenth French Corps, it remained in reserve for a few days at the disposal of the Allied commander-in-chief. On July 11th, the entire division was placed at the disposition of the Tenth Army, and between the 12th and 15th moved to the area of Dammartin-en-Goële. On the latter date it was attached to the Twentieth French Corps, and orders were received to proceed that night to the sector of the corps in the line southwest of Soissons. At this time preliminary instructions were received for the attack of the 18th.

During the night of July 15th-16th, the 1st and 2nd Infantry Brigades, the 1st Regiment of Engineers, and other dismounted elements of the division were moved by French trucks to the vicinity of Palesnes. The personnel and material of the light artillery units were also transported by trucks on the same night, while the howitzer regiment and all horsed elements commenced the march to the corps area, the latter billeting in the vicinity of Crépy-en-Valois on July 16th. On that day Division Headquarters was established at Mortefontaine.

It was not until late on the 16th that the final order for the attack was received from the Twentieth Corps,—Operations Order No. 227, July 16th, 1918. But during the night a warning order was sent out prior to the distribution, early on the 17th, of Field Order No. 27, providing for the attack. The front line battalions were moved forward in the night from their bivouacs near Palesnes to bivouacs in the vicinity of Mortefontaine, and reconnaissance of the division sector by all arms commenced, continuing throughout the 17th. Owing to the exhausted condition of the men and animals it was necessary to improvise motor transportation for the movement of the heavy guns into position. This was accomplished on the night of the 16th.

In the attack order, the road running from La Glaux Farm northeast through Tilleul de la Glaux, at an average distance of about two and a half kilometres from the front line, was designated as the first objective for the division. Another two kilometres beyond this road lay the second objective, extending along the eastern limits of the ravine east of Montplaisir Farm, and the village of Missy-aux-Bois, and Cravençon Farm. The final objective for the day was the hostile position along the high ground just beyond the Paris-Soissons road at a distance of six kilometres from the line of departure, to which the axis of progression ran east-southeast. Narrowing slightly at the first objective, the sector beyond diminished to approximately two kilometres.

The first line battalions were to cross the front line, lying north and south through La Grosse Croix slightly east of Cutry, at H-hour—4:35 a.m.—under cover of a rolling barrage, but without artillery preparation. Concurrently, the support battalions were to move forward and take up positions east of the line of departure, thence following the assaulting units without losing distance as the advance progressed. The assault battalions were to organise each objective thoroughly as it was taken, paying special attention to the proper employment of the accompanying machine gun units—one company with each battalion, and brigade battalions in close support. When the second line battalions had progressed beyond the second objective, the third line battalions were to move forward and organise the first objective along the road from La Glaux Farm and Tilleul de la Glaux. The attack was to progress at the rate of one hundred meters in two minutes to the first objective, and one hundred meters in three minutes thereafter, while a standing barrage was to rest in front of the first objective twenty minutes, and in front of the second objective forty-five minutes. The customary " battle barrage" to prevent straggling was to be composed of a cordon of military police established along the line St. Pierre-Aigle through Cutry.

On the night of the 17th the assaulting units were with great difficulty got into their positions over trails and fields made heavy by a downpour of rain. The Germans had drenched the ravine of the little Ru de Retz behind the line of departure with mustard gas so thoroughly that only the most careful forethought as to the selection of routes enabled the troops to be moved forward without losses. The entire 1st Division was in position, however, well before H-hour. With a sector about two and one-half kilometres in width at the line of departure, it was formed for the attack with brigades abreast and regiments in line, each regiment echeloned in depth of three battalions. The 1st and 2nd Infantry Brigades divided the sector about equally, the line from the south edge of Cutry to Tilleul de la Glaux and thence to the northern edge of Missy-aux-Bois, and the head of the ravine southwest of Ploissy marking their interior limits.

The brigade sub-sectors were also equally divided between the 18th, 16th, 26th, and 28th Infantry Regiments, which were placed in line in the order given from right to left. Owing to the fact that the

Ru de Retz and the ravines east of Riversau Farm and north of Cutry were under a heavy and constant shell fire and filled with yperite gas, both the assault and support battalions were stationed east of the Ru de Retz, while the third line battalions were formed west of the Riversau Farm ravine and the Ru de.Retz.

The third line battalions of the two interior regiments composed the brigade reserves, to each of which were attached one company of engineers. The division reserve was formed by the remainder of the 1st Engineers, posted in the valley west of Mortefontaine, together with the 1st Machine Gun Battalion, on the road in the ravine northeast of that place. The headquarters of the 1st and 2nd Infantry Brigades were established at Le Murger Farm and in the quarry north of Riversau Farm, respectively. The divisional artillery was emplaced in the region of Soucy and Coeuvres-et-Valsery, going into position during the night of July 17th-18th. The corps was to add one subgroupment of 105's or 155's, reinforced by the 253rd Field Artillery Regiment (French). Finally Groupment XI of French Heavy Tanks, composed of four groups, each of three batteries of four tanks, was attached to the division.

Of the other units composing the Twentieth Corps, the 1st Moroccan Division, with headquarters at Vivières, had occupied its post in line for a fortnight. No problem confronted it in taking up its assault position. But not so the 2nd Division. Placed in line near Château Thierry in the beginning of June, it had not been relieved till July 6th-8th. Heavily engaged during the early part of this period it had, like the 1st Division, rendered excellent service, culminating in a brilliant operation which resulted in the taking of Vaux on July 1st. Upon its relief, it had been withdrawn to the second line southwest of Château Thierry behind the 26th U. S. Division, which had relieved it in the sector between Vaux and Bouresches. While in this position it was constantly engaged in work upon the defences, and was subjected to shelling by the enemy's heavy guns, so that it enjoyed but little rest.

Intimation of its probable employment north of the Ourcq was first received by the division on July 14th when the 2nd Field Artillery Brigade was directed to proceed during the night by a forced march to Betz, whence it continued to Taillefontaine. On July 15th important changes occurred in the command, Major-General James G. Harbord, formerly commanding the 4th Brigade (Marines), assuming command of the division, vice Major-General Omar Bundy, transferred to command of the Sixth U. S. Corps. Major-General John A. Lejeune, U.S.M.C., succeeded to the command of the 4th Brigade, while Brigadier-General Hanson E. Ely succeeded Major-General Edward M. Lewis in command of the 3rd Brigade, the latter being transferred to the command of the 30th Division on the British Front.

During the night of the 15th orders were received attaching the division to the Third U. S. Corps and directing it to proceed to the area of the Twentieth French Corps on the front of the Tenth Army. The following night the dismounted elements of the division were transported by *camions*[2] *via* Marcilly, St. Soupplets and Palesnes to the vicinity of Pierrefonds, Retheuil, and Taillefontaine, the horsed elements marching during the night. The move was a difficult one. Only with the utmost difficulty, and after many misdirections, was the ultimate destination of the division finally discovered by the staff. Division Headquarters was established at Carrefour-de-Nemours, about four kilometres north of Villers-Cotterets in the Forêt de Retz.

Ordered to proceed by marching to their positions in line, the troops started at dawn of the 17th. The infantry columns marched throughout the day, arriving in the vicinity of Division Headquarters between 6 and 10 p.m., with the men much exhausted. The day had been intensely warm, with food and water lacking, but no halt for rest was possible, as the attack was to be launched at dawn of the 18th. To add to the hardships of the weary troops a thunderstorm broke upon them during the night. Without the slightest opportunity for reconnaissance they pressed on toward their battle positions on the eastern edge of the Forêt de Retz.

A copy of the attack order having been obtained at Corps Headquarters in Retheuil on the night of July 16th, Field Order No. 15 was prepared during the early hours of the morning and distributed on the 17th, while the troops were marching toward their position.

The line of departure assigned to the division, which was on the right of the Moroccans, lay approximately along the Laie des Fourneaux, with the left boundary of the sector at the junction between the Laie des Fourneaux and the Laie du Fond d'Argent, and the right boundary two and a half kilometres to the south. The enemy was still occupying the eastern edge of the Forêt de Retz in front of Verte Feuille Farm., distant about a kilometre. The three successive objectives assigned in orders lay along north and south lines marked by Beaurepaire Farm, the ravine of Vauxcastille, and Vierzy, at distances of

---

2. French term for motor-trucks.

PLAYING CARDS UNDER THE SHELLS

three, four and a half, and six kilometres, respectively, from the line of departure. At the second objective a deep and difficult ravine stretched across the entire sector. The axis of progression, running northeast to the first objective, turned east to the second, and bent sharply southeast to the final objective at Vierzy, which lay at the centre of the sector.

The northern, or left third of the division sector was assigned to the 4th, and the remainder to the 3rd Brigade, thus placing in line from left to right the 5th Marines, 9th Infantry, and the 23rd Infantry, each regiment in column of battalions echeloned in depth. The 2nd Engineers and 4th Machine Gun Battalion constituted the division reserve, and the 6th Marines a special corps reserve with its three battalions stationed at the Christine Cross Roads, quarry Amélie, and the cross roads southeast of Montgobert, respectively. One battalion of engineers and the divisional machine gun battalion were posted at the Ventes-Gagnier cross roads, and one battalion of engineers at the De la Blauve cross roads. The 2nd Field Artillery Brigade, reinforced by the 268th French Field Artillery Regiment, was directed to support the attack from the region of St. Pierre-Aigle, where it had taken up positions on the morning of July 16th under orders of the Twentieth Corps.

The 15th Field Artillery was to support the 3rd Brigade, and the 12th Field Artillery the 5th Marines. A groupment of heavy French tanks, consisting of three groups, each of three batteries of three or four tanks each, was assigned to the 3rd Brigade, and a similar number to the 5th Marines. The battle barrage was fixed along the line Puiseux-Fonds Douchards. Without artillery preparation, but following closely a rolling barrage, the infantry was to advance at the rate of one hundred meters in two minutes. Brief halts were prescribed at both intermediate objectives.

Although the division went into line under circumstances of peculiar difficulty, which was partly responsible for the confusion and disorder within the division itself, one finds little to criticise in the operations of the corps which directed the movement. It is to be recalled that precision of movement on the part of individual divisions was of secondary importance to the element of surprise in the general attack. Much credit is due the division, however, for the lack of complaint and the good spirit with which both officers and men bore the ordeal, especially since they could not at the time understand the necessity for the extraordinary hardships to which they were subjected.

7: The Twentieth Corps, July 18th

The terrain within the sector of the Twentieth Corps was peculiarly well adapted to defence, and if it had been held with resolution from the first by a larger force than the enemy actually found available, it would have presented almost insurmountable difficulties to the assailants. The high and bare plateau which lies west of Soissons and south of the Aisne is cut by numerous deep and wooded ravines which generally lie transversely to the approaches from the west. Few roads cross this plateau toward the east. On July 18th, 1918, the many little villages and clusters of farmhouses huddled in the ravines all contained solid buildings of masonry construction converted with the accustomed skill of the enemy into strong points in his system of defence.

The ravines which lay within the corps sector and on its flanks, within mutual supporting distance of each other, concealed machine gun nests, disposed according to the latest German methods, enabling the enemy to cover every approach with dense bands of fire. Forward guns were scattered broadcast through the fields of high-standing wheat. Particularly in the ravines about Missy-aux-Bois, Vierzy, and Ploisy, and farther to the east on the slopes of the plateau itself the enemy found ample cover for large numbers of both light and heavy guns.

Especially well adapted to defence were the positions of Berzy-le-Sec, Buzancy, and Villemontoire, which stood like powerful bastions along the eastern edge of the plateau and offered positions of great natural strength to the defenders. Upon these points the enemy's whole system of defence within the sector was based. Viewed at a distance from the west they disclosed to the eye no outstanding features of strength over and above the ordinary village or group of buildings. Closer inspection, however, soon revealed their true nature. From the front they seemed to lie upon the even surface of the great plain extending up to them from the west. From the rear they were seen to stand high upon the crests that marked the eastern edge of the plateau, balanced on the brink of the chasm-like ravines. The dead space that lay behind them afforded perfect cover for the German guns.

Relatively to the rest of the Allied attacking line, however, the terrain in its sector was favourable to the Twentieth Corps. Difficult as were the successive positions which it was called upon to assail, they were less difficult than those confronting either the corps on its left or that on its right. Missy-aux-Bois and Vierzy, lying on its boundaries, were indeed serious obstacles. They were but characteristic of the terrain throughout the whole extent of the adjoining sectors. Even without resistance, progress in those sectors must necessarily have been slow, owing to the rugged nature of the ground. Likewise, within the sector of the Twentieth Corps itself, the most difficult ground for the earlier stages of the attack fell, not to the Americans, but to the Moroccans in the centre. Viilemontoire and Buzancy, which these latter were called upon to take, were undoubtedly the most difficult to reach and storm of all the hostile strong points confronting the Twentieth Corps. The difficulties encountered by the French divisions on the flanks of the Americans must not be underestimated by those who seek to understand their relatively tardy progress.

Some of those who were present have graphically described the hours preceding the attack. For many miles in rear of the assault positions the dark and narrow lanes seethed with life. What appeared an unprecedented throng of struggling humanity swarmed in apparent confusion. Men, animals, and a vast number of guns, tanks, and transport vehicles seemed to be inextricably mingled and hopelessly lost in the dark, the mud, and the veritable maze of unmarked forest routes. But as the struggling groups pressed eastward toward the front lines, confusion gradually gave way, and by some means a measure of order evolved out of the chaos in spite of the dense fog that had succeeded the downpour of the earlier night.

Then came the dawn preceding the hour of the assault, and the sunrise, lancing its rays through the fog, soon dispelled the mists which hung for a while over the tree-tops. Broad *vistas* of the intervening spaces appeared through the trees. Vast expanses of ripened wheat, dripping with the damp, glistened in the morning light. Only the explosion of an occasional German shell broke the strange, unnatural calm, a calm so marked, so intense, that even now men recall the song of the birds about them. Indeed, in the peaceful scene that spread before them, so quiet after the night's noise and confusion, there was little to suggest the impending storm soon to break in fury.

Forbidden to reply to the casual lire of the enemy, the Allies had not fired a shot during the early morning. At last a friendly shell shrieked overhead, then another, and another,—soon followed by the simultaneous crash and rumble of a thousand pieces. The earth seemed to reel under the concussion. Thus was H-hour announced, while the infantry waited breathlessly in position, or toiled through the tangled forest toward the front. The barrage rolled forward on schedule time. The assaulting troops followed closely all along the line of the Twentieth Corps from Laversine on the north toward Longpont on the south. With several hundred heavy tanks in front of them, they advanced without hesitation. Almost no hostile artillery fire fell on them for a considerable time. Infantry resistance was feeble. To the enemy the attack came as a complete surprise.

Advancing more rapidly than the Moroccans, the 1st Brigade took its first objective at 5:30 a.m., and by 7 a.m. had seized its half of the second objective. The 2nd Brigade, also advancing, more rapidly than the French on its flank, occupied the whole of its second objective by 7:30, despite the machine gun fire developed from Missy-aux-Bois and the part of the Missy ravine opposite the 153rd French Division on the left. But from Missy-aux-Bois eastward the country became more difficult and resistance increased. The enemy's guns now came into action, and every wheat-field contained hidden machine guns which were not only almost impossible to locate, but were operated with the stubbornness of desperation.

Owing to the continued failure of the 153rd French Division, adjoining the corps sector on the left, to come up abreast of the 1st U. S. Division, the 2nd Brigade was unable to advance beyond the second objective. At every attempt it was enfiladed from the north and northeast. But advancing with the Moroccans on the right abreast of it, the 1st Brigade reached the final objective with slight loss. With complete liaison established between the 18th Infantry and the Moroccans, this brigade was compelled to refuse its left in order to connect with the 2nd Brigade in position along the Missy ravine. This necessity brought the 16th Infantry on its left under the same fire to which the 2nd Brigade was subjected, resulting in heavy losses. Thus on the night of the 1 8th the front line of the division, extending along the Missy ravine past Missy, bent forward to the final objective, a distance of a kilometre to the east. It connected with the line of the Moroccans immediately north of Chaudun. Contact was finally established on the left with the 153rd Division, and the entire line consolidated.

At 7:30 a.m. Division Headquarters had moved from Mortefontaine to the quarry immediately west of Coeuvres, where the reserve was also stationed. The attack had been closely followed up and supported by the artillery. One battalion, 18th Infantry, in reserve, had been moved to Dommiers, whence it was to move in trucks in support of the Second French Cavalry Corps in case the hostile line should break.

103

SEARCHING THE GERMAN DEAD AFTER THE CAPTURE OF A TRENCH

The day had been a most successful one in spite of the failure of the left brigade to reach the final objective. Approximately two thousand prisoners, including seventy-five officers, were taken by the division. Many machine guns were seized and turned upon the enemy. In one quarry an entire battalion of five hundred men with its commander was captured. About thirty field guns (77's and 150's) were captured in the Missy ravine and neighbouring positions. The losses of the day approximated a total of not over fifteen hundred officers and men.

As we have seen, the 2nd Division attacked on the other side of the Moroccans. It did not have the advantage which the other divisions of the corps possessed in being able to make reconnaissance and bring the assault troops into position in an orderly way. Only by the most unusual exertion did the front line units manage to arrive in time to participate in the attack. All during the night great confusion reigned among the troops. The traffic congestion compelled the infantry to follow the ditches which paralleled the trails, thus stringing out the columns and causing both the intermingling of units and straggling. Men cursed as they toiled on. Others too weary to march farther, threw themselves upon the ground, from which they were urged to their feet with difficulty. Teamsters cracked their whips and shouted; tanks panted over the greasy routes and crushed their way forward; light and heavy guns stalled in the mud or became entangled in the thickets, sweating teams labouring at the traces. Staff cars, trucks, and motor-cycles innumerable added to the difficulties of the men.

Notwithstanding all this, however, the 1st Battalion, 9th Infantry, relieved the front line battalion of the 48th French Infantry before midnight and attacked in good order at H-hour. The leading elements of the 5th Marines on the left, and of the 23rd Infantry on the right, were deploying as the barrage fell. But the machine-gun battalions and companies, and the 37mm. and Stokes mortar platoons with their transport, were inextricably involved in the traffic congestion in the rear, and failed to arrive in time to accompany the infantry. The assault was made with the musket and bayonet supported by the artillery.

The troops advanced over ground which rose gently from the line of departure toward the northeast. Wheat-fields stretched as far as the eye could see, with lurking machine gunners carefully concealed in the tall grain. In the centre of the sector, a kilometre or more in advance of the first objective, a group of strongly fortified buildings stood as an outpost at Verte Feuille Farm. Beyond this formidable obstacle was the stronger post of Beaurepaire Farm, marking the line of the first objective itself. Here, advancing with a rush, the 2nd Battalion, 9th Infantry, reached the objective within fifteen minutes, and the 3rd Battalion of the same regiment followed in close support. The 2nd Battalion, 23rd Infantry, soon arrived on the right, followed closely by the 3rd Battalion, both of them having been misdirected by the French guides in getting into position.

The left battalion of the other, or 4th, brigade (1st Battalion, 5th Marines), which was actually deploying when the barrage fell, at once advanced north of the Paris-Maubeuge road with its left on the Laie du Chrétiennette. More tardy in its arrival at the line of departure, the 2nd Battalion, on the right of the brigade, and in liaison on the right with the left of the 9th Infantry, moved forward with one company south of the Paris-Maubeuge road. Two of its companies, misdirected by their French guides, became mingled with the 1st Battalion, and the remaining company failed to rejoin the battalion until late in the day. Notwithstanding this, however, the 2nd Battalion overran Verte Feuille Farm, soon after the 9th Infantry on its right had taken Beaurepaire. In its progress it lost contact with the 9th Infantry, and its left, crossing in rear of the 1st Battalion in its front, worked over into the sector of the Moroccans.

From Beaurepaire Farm on, all connection between the 2nd Division and the 38th French Division on its right was lost. By 7 a.m. the 3rd Brigade overcame stubborn resistance in the Vauxcastille ravine and the 23rd Infantry moved forward independently of the French. The enemy, however, still held out with fine determination in Vierzy. Communication between Division Headquarters and the front lines had failed, and General Harbord went forward in person to reconnoitre the situation. In so doing, he met, wholly by chance, the commanding general of the 3rd Brigade, General Ely, whose headquarters had recently been advanced to Beaurepaire Farm. From him he learned of the situation in his front, and promptly issued orders for the resumption of the attack at 4:30 p.m. in the direction, of the Bois de Hartennes and the Château Thierry road.

General Ely, however, did not meet with as much luck as his superior. In the confusion of the battle he experienced such difficulty in getting back to his headquarters that it was 4:30, the attack hour, before he could communicate his orders to his regimental commanders, and both of these then declared it an impossibility to resume the attack before 6:00. The tank commander insisted upon a further delay of one hour. It was a case of making the best of a confused situation

in which haste was imperative, and General Ely directed each unit to attack as soon as possible, but in no case later than 6:00 p.m.

To comply with this order was a difficult task. The following was the situation. By 4:30 p.m. the 1st and 2nd Battalions, 5th Marines, had succeeded in organising the left of the line along the second objective, the 3rd Battalion remaining in support at Verte Feuille Farm, to which point it had been moved forward about noon. On the right of the division sector the 1st and 2nd Battalions, 9th Infantry, and the 2nd and 1st Battalions, 23rd Infantry, in the order named from left to right, were in possession of the Vauxcastille ravine and the slopes in advance of it overlooking Vierzy. The 3rd Battalion, 9th Infantry, was in support, while the 3rd Battalion, 23rd Infantry, remained as brigade reserve in the woods at the line of departure. For the new attack it was ordered that the 2nd Battalion, 5th Marines, supported by the 1st Battalion, 9th Infantry, and the 2nd Battalion, 9th Infantry, supported by the 3rd Battalion, should advance within the sector north of Vierzy, while the 2nd and 1st Battalions, 23rd Infantry, supported by the 1st Battalion, 5th Marines, was directed to take the town itself. Fifteen tanks were to accompany the 9th, and an equal number the 23rd Infantry, and each regiment was to be supported by a regiment of light artillery.

As might have been expected under the circumstances, the attack was delivered in a very ragged manner. Liaison between the artillery and infantry had been lost after the progression of the latter from the first objective. The artillery had moved forward, but upon the direction of the corps it was ordered to execute counter-battery fire, so that the infantry was compelled to make its second attack without the cover of the promised barrage. Only a few machine guns had managed to reach the front line, and the support which they could offer to the attackers may be considered negligible. On the right, the 1st Battalion, 5th Marines, which had been drawn out of the line on the left and moved with great difficulty to the Vauxcastille ravine, advanced, about 7:15 p.m., into Vierzy ahead of the 23rd Infantry. In its attack it was assisted by the French tanks. While engaged in and about the town it was passed by the 2nd Battalion and elements of the 1st Battalion of the 23rd Infantry, which pushed on with terrific losses to the high ground east of the town, where progress ceased about 8:30 p.m. Led by Colonel Upton, in person, the 2nd Battalion, 9th Infantry, advanced at 7:30 p.m., and after proceeding about a kilometre to the final objective was brought to a halt with its left enfiladed by machine guns in the Bois Léchelle.

The 2nd Battalion, 5th Marines, and the 1st Battalion, 9th Infantry, also encountered heavy fire, and veering somewhat to the left were brought to a halt after reaching the line of the final objective in front of the Bois Léchelle. At this point a detachment of six French tanks, moving to the rear from the Bois Léchelle, brought down upon the right of the Moroccans and the 5th Marines a violent and long sustained fire from the hostile artillery, which subjected the Marines to heavy losses and compelled the Moroccans to withdraw some distance to the. cover of an old line of trenches. Resistance was increasing all along the front, night had fallen, and the enemy flares showed that the line of the 2nd Division formed a marked salient within the hostile position. With both flanks uncovered further progress was impossible. The front line units had become intermingled and disorganised. The sharp turn to the southeast after passing the second objective had resulted in considerable confusion among the elements of the 9th and 23rd Infantry, and mingled with the 23rd Infantry on the extreme right were elements of the 1st Battalion, 5th Marines, while on the left, elements of the 2nd Battalion, 5th Marines, were mangled with the 9th Infantry.

Energetic measures were now undertaken to reorganise the front line. About 9 p.m. the order was given to dig in, a task which was accomplished with the aid of the 2nd Engineers. Machine guns had begun to arrive and these were employed in the consolidation of the position. The 3rd Battalion, 5th Marines, and the whole of the 6th Marines, which had been moved forward to the woods south of Beaurepaire Farm about 6 a.m., Remained in reserve during the night.

Thus the 18th of July closed with the Twentieth Corps established throughout its entire length upon the line of its final objective for the day. So far as it was concerned, the first day of the offensive had been a successful one in every respect. The two American divisions advancing ahead of the French divisions on their exterior flanks, and at no time in rear of the Moroccans in the centre, had driven a marked salient into the enemy's line, which had been everywhere forced back. The 1st U. S. Division had functioned like clockwork. The 2nd U. S. Division, though labouring from the start under enormous disadvantages and suffering from considerable confusion, had maintained its schedule in the advance. The Moroccans had lived up to their reputation.

From the standpoint of its execution, however, the attack of the 2nd U. S. Division disclosed many defects in technique, which were to be remedied, in part, the following day. It is not too much to say that liaison within the division broke down completely, and that the usual means of communication failed to function from the first. Generals and colonels delivered their orders in person. One of the assault battalions of the 5th Marines, starting late through unavoidable circumstances, was badly oriented throughout the day, and several of its elements got lost. In the haste of the advance the intermediate positions were carelessly and inadequately organised and consolidated. Over the action as a whole the division command had no control whatever, nor any accurate knowledge of its progress except that obtained by the casual encounter of the division commander and a brigade commander on the battlefield.

There was one culpable error committed, moreover, which was repeated on many occasions during the war. Misinformation as to the progress of units within adjoining sectors, and tidings of a supposed advance of French cavalry, indicating a complete breakthrough, were purposely disseminated among the attacking units. This, although designed to spur them on to redoubled efforts, only caused unnecessary sacrifices among the men, and later aroused their suspicion and protests. It is to be regretted that, as usual in such cases, it is not possible to determine the source of the "mistake."

8: The Twentieth Corps, July 19th

As the First French Corps on the left of the Twentieth approached its objective of July 18th, it met increased resistance from the enemy, who was making desperate efforts to maintain his positions along the southern bank of the Aisne west of the town of Soissons, on which his resistance was based. The obstacles in the path of the 153rd French Division had been from the first so serious as to slow up its advance considerably, complicating and rendering most difficult the task of the Twentieth. The Twentieth therefore could not press its advance straight toward the east without exposing its left flank to possible disaster.

On the night of July 18th, however, it was ordered to resume the attack at 4 a.m. the following morning. At 1:35 a.m., July 19th, Field Order No. 28, 1st U. S. Division, was issued. The line Buzancy-Berzy-le-Sec was designated as the objective for the day. From the position of the 2nd Brigade along the eastern edge of the Missy-aux-Bois ravine to Berzy-le-Sec was four kilometres, while Buzancy was at a distance of six kilometres from the 1st Brigade. Upon this objective the division was to consolidate, facing northeast, in order to protect the ex-

Capture of a German "Minenwerfer"

posed corps flank. The line from Missy-aux-Bois to the southern edge of the pond south of Aconin Farm was indicated as the interior limit of the two brigades.

The task set the 1st U. S. Division for the attack was a serious one. Not only had the terrain become more difficult, but during the night the enemy had brought two first-class divisions into the line opposite. As in the case of the preceding day, there was to be no artillery preparation for the attack. A barrage was to stand forty-five minutes while the 2nd Brigade moved up abreast of the 1st, and was then to roll forward at the rate of one hundred meters in three minutes. Tanks were to precede the infantry. The battalion of the 28th Infantry in division reserve was placed at the disposal of the 2nd Brigade, while the battalion of the 18th Infantry which had been sent to Dommiers for the support of the cavalry was held there as part of the division reserve. The entire division reserve was directed not to move. Division Headquarters remained in the quarry five hundred meters west of Coeuvres.

Promptly at 4 a.m. the attack was launched. The French tanks, which had rendered excellent service the preceding day, failed to clear the way on the left, being unable to penetrate into the ravine of Ploisy, and again the 153rd French Division failed to take that part of the Missy-aux-Bois ravine which lay in its sector. After encountering violent artillery and machine gun fire from Ploisy and farther to the north, the 2nd Brigade was brought to a complete halt short of the Paris road after advancing less than a kilometre from the Missy ravine. Upon reaching the ravine at Chazelle the 1st Brigade found its left much exposed on account of the failure of the 2nd Brigade to advance, and after sustaining heavy casualties was also compelled to halt. Considerable confusion arose along the front line, so that the remainder of the morning and the afternoon were consumed in reorganising, and in re-establishing contact between the various units, and with the 153rd French Division.

During the day a new effort was organised, set for 5:30 p.m., with the object of advancing the left of the line. The 153rd French Division was ordered to press forward, and the 1st U. S. Division was to establish itself on the line from the western edge of the Ploisy ravine to the head of the Chazelle ravine. Should the 153rd French Division advance beyond this line the 1st U. S. Division was to conform to its movements in liaison with the Moroccans on the right.

The attack was successfully conducted by the 1st U. S. Division, though at terrific cost to the 2nd Brigade. This brigade reached the western edge of the Ploisy ravine, but again was enfiladed by machine gun fire from the north. The hostile artillery on the eastern slopes of the plateau was very active. The 1st Brigade advanced slightly beyond Chazelle. When night fell the line was marked by the Ferme du Mt. de Courmelles, the western edge of the Ploisy ravine, and Chazelle, with close connection established on both flanks. Casualties probably numbered three thousand, but an additional thousand prisoners were taken, including about thirty-five officers. Twenty more field guns were also taken at Ploisy and Chazelle.

In the centre, the Moroccans advanced their left abreast of the 1st U. S. Division. But their right was retarded, and beyond them, with both its flanks exposed, the 2nd U. S. Division had met with only partial success. The corps order for the attack had not been received at Division Headquarters until 2 a.m. It had therefore been necessary to proceed regardless of the plan of the corps. The troops holding the line east of Vierzy were found incapable of further efforts and the division reserve alone remained available for the attack, but this could not be brought up by 4 a.m. Not till 3 a.m. could Field Order No. 15, setting forth the amended plan of attack, be published.

The line Hartennes-et-Taux-Bois d'Hartennes-Bois de Cornerois, including a part of the Soissons-Château Thierry highway, at a distance of about four kilometres from Vierzy, was designated as the objective for the 2nd Division. Artillery preparation was to commence at 6 a.m., while the assaulting troops were to cross the front line at 7 a.m. and follow a rolling barrage. The 6th Marines and the 6th Machine Gun Battalion, preceded by tanks, were to make the assault, with the 1st Battalion, 2nd Engineers, and the 4th Machine Gun Battalion in reserve, while the 3rd Brigade and 5th Marines were to remain in their positions of the preceding night. Division Headquarters was established at Beaurepaire Farm, and both brigade headquarters at Vierzy.

The order of attack was received at 5 a.m. at Beaurepaire Farm by the 6th Marines, where the regiment had been posted in reserve the preceding night. Although no time was lost it proved impossible for the regiment to attack at 7 a.m. Marching to Vierzy three kilometres under shell fire the regiment was deployed, still under fire and in the open, with the 2nd and 1st Battalions in the front line, on the left and right, respectively, followed by the 3rd Battalion in support at a distance of a kilometre. As it moved forward under hostile observation across the open wheat-fields, the regiment, preceded by slow-moving tanks, was compelled to advance through a hostile counter-barrage which inflicted serious losses upon it, and it was 9 a.m. before it reached the front line at a distance of a kilometre or more beyond the town. It continued to advance, however, till, a kilometre farther on, at about 10:30 a.m., it was driven to seek cover in a line of incomplete German trenches on the western outskirts of Tigny.

There it remained throughout the day under heavy shell fire, the 3rd Battalion reinforcing the front line and the 1st Battalion, 2nd Engineers, becoming the support. Enfiladed by machine gun fire on both flanks, and subjected to severe artillery fire, its estimated losses were 70% of its effective strength. During the afternoon the 38th French Division moved up abreast on the right and the Moroccans on the left, thus relieving the situation to some extent, but no further advance on its part was possible. Indeed, the relief of the entire 2nd U. S. Division now became imperative. The 9th Infantry reported an effective strength of but three hundred and thirty-three men, and the 23rd Infantry but twenty-seven officers and fourteen hundred and seventy-eight men in line.

A total loss of thirty-seven hundred and eighty-eight, including one hundred and fifty-four officers, was reported for the division. Accordingly, on the night of the 19th at the request of the division commander, the division was relieved; by the 58th Colonial Division, and withdrawn to the woods west of Verte Feuille Farm, where it was stationed as corps reserve.

The following day, when its condition became better known, it was relieved, less artillery, from duty with the Twentieth Corps, and moved to the Nanteuil rest area in reserve of the Tenth Army. The 2nd Field Artillery Brigade was attached successively to the 58th Colonial and the 12th French Divisions, with which last it continued in action until the night of July 25th.

During its presence in the line the 2nd U. S. Division had advanced over eight kilometres against the most stubborn resistance, almost always ahead of the units on its flanks. Besides a large number of guns of various calibres and much material, it had captured over three thousand prisoners. The rest it was about to enjoy was well earned.

9: The 1st Division carries on

With its position forming the apex of the salient which the Twentieth Corps had driven into the German position by its attacks of the 18th and 19th, the 1st U. S. Division was called upon for further efforts after the 2nd Division was relieved. East of Ploisy the strong-hold of Berzy-le-Sec, hidden from view by a slight rise in the plateau, remained to be taken. Skilfully organised as a strong point, the village and surrounding ravine commanded the country beyond, which sloped steeply to the Soissons-Château Thierry road, as well as all the communications leading to that road from the west.

In the original plan of attack Berzy-le-Sec had been included within the sector of the 153rd French Division, but that division was neither in a position to take it on July 20th, nor was it able to make the attempt, for other reasons pointed out by its commander. During the night of the 19th, therefore, the existing plans were recast, and orders were issued for the 1st U. S. Division to assault the town the following day. The 2nd Battalion, 18th Infantry, which had been stationed as division reserve southwest of the Ploisy ravine on the Missy-aux-Bois road, was placed at the disposition of the 2nd Brigade for the attack. The advance was to be preceded by a powerful artillery preparation of two hours. A barrage was to stand from 1:15 to 2:00 p.m. along a line east of Ploisy and Chazelle and roll forward at the latter hour at the rate of a hundred meters in four minutes.

Thoroughly reorganised during the night, the division attacked on the 20th in accordance with the plan, but failed to take Berzy-le-Sec on the left or to reach the Château Thierry road on the right. Again through the failure of the 153rd French Division to advance, the 2nd Brigade suffered serious casualties from enfilade fire delivered from the north. But on the right, in close liaison with the Moroccans, the 1st Brigade crossed the railroad and advanced to the vicinity of Bois Gérard, Visigneux, and Aconin Farm, refusing its left flank to connect with the 2nd Brigade.

At nightfall the 28th Infantry dug in on the plateau in front of Berzy-le-Sec, and the 26th Infantry along the road from Berzy-le-Sec to Chazelle. About a thousand casualties were suffered during the day and only a few prisoners were taken.

The Moroccans on the right had crossed the railway and entered the Bois Gérard. On the left the 153rd French Division had failed to advance beyond the Ferme du Mt. de Courmelles. A new attack for the 21st was ordered by the corps. During the night the 1st Moroccan Division was relieved by the 87th, and the 153rd French Division by the 69th French Division. The necessity of maintaining liaison with these two divisions, of which the first was about two kilometres in advance of the second, complicated the task of the 1st Division

HELPING THE WOUNDED

enormously. With the Soissons-Château Thierry road and the wooded heights north of Buzancy as its objective, it was to attack at 4:45 a.m. under cover of a rolling barrage. No artillery preparation was prescribed. The 2nd Battalion, 18th Infantry, which had delivered the attack on the 21st, was to be the division reserve.

The commander of the 69th French Division, just arrived in the sector, declared his utter inability to attack at so early an hour, and demanded an artillery preparation of three hours. This delay prevented the 2nd Brigade from advancing until 8:30 a.m., but the 1st Brigade moved forward behind the barrage at the appointed hour, and the whole attack, though disjointed, proved most successful. Advancing with its left refused, the 1st Brigade reached its objective on the heights north of Buzancy in spite of a heavy flanking fire from the north, and the 2nd Brigade took Berzy-le-Sec, making important captures of men and guns. The remainder of the day was spent in consolidating the line and pushing forward patrols. At nightfall the line embraced the heights north of Berzy-le-Sec, the Château Thierry road south of the Sucrerie, and the heights north of Visigneux. In this position the division was notified that the promised relief during the night was impossible, due to inability to bring up a fresh division. Throughout the night casualties were sustained by machine gun fire from the north, and from long-range artillery fire from the Missy-aux-Bois ravine in the left rear.

As the 87th French Division had failed to take Buzancy, no further progress was possible, and the following day was devoted to the straightening of the line, which involved the taking of the Sucrerie by the 26th Infantry. Casualties on the 22nd were light. During the night of July 22nd-23rd, the division was relieved, including one-third of the artillery. The following night the remainder of the artillery was relieved, and the entire division assembled in the Dammartin rest area in reserve of the Tenth Army, where it was to remain until, with the 2nd U. S. Division, it was transferred on the 31st to the Fourth U. S. Corps with headquarters at Neufchâteau.

During the five days that the 1st U. S. Division was engaged with the Twentieth French Corps, it had progressed eleven kilometres and had at all times been a leader in the advance of the Tenth Army. Having reached and crossed the great highway to Château Thierry in the lead of all other units, the position which it finally reached on the plateau above the Crise, where it was relieved, dominated the city of Soissons itself. The division had attained the objective set for it, and had captured about three thousand eight hundred prisoners and seventy guns. Its losses were enormous, being reported as approximately a thousand killed, with a total of seven thousand casualties, including over sixty *per cent* of the commissioned personnel. The 16th and 18th Infantry lost all their field officers except their colonels; the 28th Infantry lost two, and the 26th Infantry all of its field officers.

10: THE SIXTH ARMY, JULY 18TH

Having followed the 1st and 2nd U. S. Divisions to their final objectives and to the point at which they were withdrawn from the line on the front of the Tenth Army, we now turn to the front Of the Sixth Army on which the other American units were engaged.

On the morning of July 18th, the Sixth Army was formed as shown in the chart. The Second French Corps held the line from the Savières River, from a point just north of the Ourcq midway between Faverolles and Ancienville, to a point south of Dammard; the Seventh French Corps continued the line to a point southwest of Hautevennes; the First U. S. Corps prolonged it to Vaux; the Thirty-Eighth French Corps from Vaux beyond Mézy; and the Third French Corps to the vicinity of Dormans. Thus the left wing, composed of the Second and Seventh French Corps, held a north and south line, while the right wing, composed of the Thirty-Eighth and Third French Corps, held the east and west line of the Marne, and the First U. S. Corps held the centre.

The mission of the Sixth Army for the 18th was to fight a holding action with its centre and right, while the left advanced in prolongation of the line of the Tenth Army on the north. The obvious purpose of its operations was to hold the enemy in position along the Marne in order that his withdrawal from that quarter might be prevented by the penetration of the Tenth Army in his rear. But, in the event the enemy should commence a withdrawal notwithstanding, the right and centre of the Sixth Army were to abandon their mere delaying action and press northward closely upon his heels. At all costs the Sixth Army was to prevent the reinforcement of the enemy's right by the transfer of troops from the left. The general plan of operations involved a nicety of adjustment and the most careful timing of movement.

According to schedule and without artillery preparation, the Second and Seventh French Corps delivered the attack at 4:35 a.m. on the 18th, advancing in prolongation of the line of the Tenth Army, and pivoting on the First U. S. Corps. Involved in their operations was the

German dead lying in the barb-wire before the American Front

4th U. S. Division, the action of which must now be traced.

Arriving in France in May, this division, less its artillery, had been assigned to a British training area under the instruction of a skeleton British division—the 16th Irish—with headquarters at Samer near Boulogne. Early in June its transfer to the Marne commenced, almost before it had entered upon its training schedule. It was an almost wholly green division, though a unit of the so-called regular establishment, for, as in the case of all the other regular divisions, its ranks were largely composed of men who had either volunteered or been drafted since the Spring of 1917. Among the non-commissioned officers only a sprinkling were of the old service.

On June 15th the division was stationed northeast of Meaux, with headquarters at Lizy-sur-Ourcq. There its units were divided for training between the 4th and 164th French Divisions of the Third French Corps. At that time the latter division was in sector, while the former occupied a second line position. In this situation the division remained until the concentration north of the Ourcq commenced, when it was assembled in reserve west of Villers-Cotterêts.

During the first stages of the counter-offensive the 7th Infantry Brigade operated under the orders of the Second French Corps, while the 8th Infantry Brigade was attached to the Seventh French Corps, but neither brigade functioned as a tactical unit and, in the main, only battalions mingled with French units were employed.

The 39th Infantry of the 7th Brigade was called upon on the afternoon of the 16th to relieve French troops in the line during the night of July 17th-18th, while the 47th Infantry remained in reserve behind Varinfroy. On the 18th it attacked on the front of the Second French Corps at 8 a.m., taking all of its objectives by 3 p.m. During the afternoon the regiment succeeded in taking Noroy, which, according to plan, should have been taken by French units.

The 8th Brigade arrived in the sector of the 164th Division, Seventh French Corps, on the night of July 16th-17th. Two battalions of the 59th Infantry were established as the division reserve, while the remaining battalion was posted at Marnen-la-Poterie as corps reserve. The 58th Infantry was assigned to an assault position and attacked at 4:35 a.m., July 18th. Without artillery preparation, the French and American troops advanced to the attack under cover of a smoke screen, taking Hautevesnes by 5, and Courchamps at 11 a.m. The American troops took the village of Chevillon, "in a splendid dash," to quote the words of the French divisional commander, then advanced very rapidly to the Sept Bois, southwest of Montmeujon. Passing beyond the wood they suddenly came under violent machine gun and artillery fire which compelled them to retire to the western edge of the Sept Bois.

On the front of the First U. S. Corps, on the other hand, little success was attained on the 18th of July. Through its relief of the 2nd U. S. Division on July 6th-8th, the 26th U. S. Division found itself in a post of vital importance on the 18th. The role which it was called upon to play was, however, accidental, inasmuch as the attack of that day was not planned until after the 26th had gone into the front line. This division, known as the Yankee Division, was composed of New England National Guard organisations. Arriving in France late in October, it had trained in the Neufchâteau area throughout the winter, and had entered the line in a quiet sector near the Chemin des Dames in March. Thus, when it was transferred to the Marne it was presumably one of the most experienced American units, having been in France longer than any other except the 1st and 42nd U. S. Divisions.

The role assigned it in the counter-offensive was indeed a difficult one. Its pivotal position, the configuration of its line, the character of the ground over which it was called upon to advance, all presented difficulties of their own. Occupying a line running generally east and west from Vaux on the right through the village of Bouresches and along the slopes overlooking Belleau and Givry, to a point west and south of the village of Torcy, it was to deliver its attack in concert with the division on its left, whose direction of advance was designed to be toward the east. Any considerable advance on its part, therefore, would necessitate a change of direction in the face of the enemy, at best a difficult manoeuvre. The difficulty was increased by a considerable curve in its own line between Vaux and Bouresches which had compelled interior units to occupy positions almost at right angles to each other. Finally, the ground over which it was to attack offered especially serious obstacles to the progress of the 52nd, or left brigade.

In the left subsector of the division, from Bouresches to Torcy, ran a narrow valley which was occupied by the enemy. The enemy also held the villages of Belleau, Givry, and Torcy along its course. Bouresches and the hills overlooking the valley from the south, on the other hand, were held by the 52nd Brigade. Behind Belleau, Givry, and Torcy rose a steep, wooded height known as Hill 193, while farther to the east a second hill—190—barred an advance in that direction. The first of these positions was a very strong one, commanding the valley in front of the American line throughout its whole length; likewise that portion of the line from Givry to Bouresches was exposed to enfilade fire from Hill 193, the seizure of which was an essential prelude to a successful advance toward the east.

The taking of Hill 193 was assigned in the corps order—No. 9, July 17th—to the 167th French Division on the left, which was to swing its line to the eastward for the purpose. To the left brigade of the 26th U. S. Division was assigned the task of taking Torcy, Givry, and Belleau, short of Hill 193, the right brigade remaining in position during the swing toward the east of the line on its left. The order was so planned as to guard against the possibility of the left elements of the 26th U. S. Division crossing the front of the division on its left and thereby obstructing its advance. Opposite the sector of the First U. S. Corps, when the attack commenced, were the 87th German Division, two regiments of the 4th Ersatz Division, and one regiment of the 201st Division. Thus the enemy line was inferior in numerical strength to that of the assailants on the day the attack opened. It continued to be thus inferior for several succeeding days.

Although an examination of the plan of the High Command for the attack of July 18th discloses the most obvious difficulties in the path of the 26th U. S. Division, these difficulties were imposed by the situation of the division rather than by the nature of the plan, which did not involve an unreasonable demand upon the 26th Division. In the original plan the 52nd Brigade was to attack at 4:35 a.m. with its two regiments—103rd and 104th—side by side in column of battalions, the 103rd Infantry on the left. The battalions selected on the eve of battle for the assault were at the time in support, which necessitated their movement into position over difficult ground during the night.

An additional cause of confusion was a late decision to throw in a second battalion of the left regiment which was to push along the railroad between Givry and Bouresches on the right of the 104th Infantry. While moving into their battle positions during the night two of these battalions crossed each other's paths in Belleau Woods behind the front line, their elements became mingled, and great confusion set in, with the not unnatural result that at the hour designated for the attack only the left battalion advanced to the assault.

Notwithstanding the miscarriage of the plan of attack and the confusion of front line elements, the village of Torcy was taken within thirty minutes by the one assaulting battalion, the attack coming as a complete surprise to the enemy. But this success on his right only

BROTHERS IN ARMS: FRENCH DRAGOON AND AMERICAN OFFICER

served to arouse the enemy to his danger in other quarters, with the result that the two battalions still struggling to gain their positions opposite his left were brought under a severe artillery fire. To assist them forward to their objectives it was arranged that they should attack under cover of a barrage at 7:30 a.m. Only the battalion of the 104th Infantry, however, advanced at this hour, the right battalion failing to move forward until 8:15 a.m., at which time it was without the support of the artillery.

During the early morning, in spite of all the difficulties in which they had been involved, the three assaulting battalions finally gained their objectives in the face of a feeble resistance on the part of inferior troops. But no sooner were their objectives gained than a very heavy fire from machine guns on Hill 193, and from hostile artillery, fell upon them, driving the troops in Givry and Belleau to the cover of the houses in those villages, and compelling the right battalion between Givry and Bouresches to abandon the position it had taken and fall back to the cover of its original lines.

It should be thoroughly understood that the advance of the 26th U. S. Division beyond its first objective on the 18th was conditioned upon the success of the 167th Division on its left. It was especially disadvantageous to the 26th U. S. Division that its orders seemed to debar it from any attempt to make good its advance by pressing beyond Torcy and Givry and on to Hill 193, which the 167th French Division had failed to seize as planned. But even in the face of its orders a serious attempt to do so would have been pardonable had notice been given to the 167th French Division. As a matter of fact, late in the evening an effort at concerted action between the two divisions was made, and a few American troops of the left battalion did actually reach the summit of the hill, but were soon withdrawn upon advice that the 167th Division was unable to support the attack.

Beyond the 39th French Division on the right of the 26th was the 3rd U. S. Division in the position already examined, with the 28th U.S. Division divided between the 39th French Division and the 125th French Division, the latter on the right of the 3rd. Neither the 3rd U.S. nor the 28th U. S. Division was engaged on the 18th of July, when the French launched their counter-attacks upon the enemy who had crossed south of the Marne to the east. On the 18th the Chief of Staff of the 3rd Division, anxious to strike a blow, vainly urged a counter-attack by the 3rd U. S. Division, supported by the 28th, against von Boehn's flank where it rested on the southern bank of the Marne.

Such an attack, however, was not in conformity with the general plan of action.

11: THE SIXTH ARMY, JULY 19TH-20TH

While the entire line north of the pivot, or First U. S. Corps, along the west face of the Marne salient, swung forward on the 18th, the greatest gains were realised by the Twentieth Corps. The failure of the Thirtieth Corps, south of the Twentieth, to advance as rapidly, caused a marked angle in the line opposite. the centre of the western face of the salient, where the new line turned sharply to the southwest past Louatre, then southward across the Ourcq east of Noroy. The angle in the centre of the line also was made more acute by the failure of the pivot to progress during the swing forward of the line to the north. Efforts were accordingly made to advance the pivot, in order to rectify the dangerous angle in the centre.

During the 19th the situation of the 3rd U. S. and 28th U. S. Divisions remained virtually unchanged. The Americans learned with regret of the passing of an apparent opportunity for a victorious counter-attack upon von Boehn's defeated left. In the Second French Corps, on the left of the Sixth Army, the 39th Infantry, 4th U. S. Division, attached to the 33rd French Division, again advanced, attacking at 4 a.m. and taking the three successive objectives set for July 19th. That night, after two days of most successful fighting, the regiment was relieved and placed in support.

In the sector of the Seventh French Corps, the elements of the 8th Brigade, 4th U. S. Division, cooperating with the 164th French Division, also met with success, assisting in taking during the day Prietz and La Grenouillère Farm. On the 20th they took Sommelans, and on the 21st they took Preteret Farm and entered the Bois de Bonnes. The following day they took Bois de Bonnes and pushed the line forward into the Bois de Châtelet. After five days of continuous heavy fighting the battalions of the 58th and 59th Infantry, which had received during that period their first experience of battle, were finally relieved from the front line. When it is recalled that the combatant strength of this one fresh American brigade probably equalled that of the entire French division to which it was attached, its influence upon the successful advance within the sector of the Seventh French Corps will not seem inconsiderable.

We return to the 26th U. S. Division, which had been checked in its advance on the 18th by the obstacle presented in Hill 193, north of Belleau and Givry. The division was compelled to await the capture of that key position by the 167th French Division on its left. Recognising fully the importance of the position, the Germans reinforced it heavily late on the 18th, and held it more firmly on the 19th than on the day before. The 167th French Division, therefore, found the magnitude of the task assigned it increased rather than diminished. All through the 19th this division struggled in vain to advance from the west, meeting the most resolute resistance at each attempt. Nor did it meet with more success on the morning of the 20th.

In the meantime the 26th U. S. Division remained idle, in so far as any organised effort to advance was concerned, for, as we have seen, under the orders of the corps, its advance, even had it been able to progress, was limited by the action of the division on its left. But on the 20th, after the repeated failure of the 167th French Division to take Hill 193, a new attack was organised, to be delivered along the entire corps front at 3 p.m., and to the 167th French Division the seizure of Hill 193 was again assigned. The 52nd Brigade, 26th U. S. Division, was to push eastward and take Hill 190, while the 51st Brigade was to support the effort of the latter with an attack on its right against the wooded region north of Vaux and east of Bouresches. After the attainment of the first objectives, the advance was to be continued by the whole corps in the direction of the Soissons-Château Thierry road. The attack of the infantry was to be preceded by an artillery preparation of an hour and a half.

The problem before the 52nd Brigade on the left of the 26th U. S. Division was no easy one. A battalion of the 104th Infantry had established itself at Torcy, facing north, with Hill 193 on its right front. In order to advance toward the east this battalion would be compelled to take a support position in rear of the battalion of the 104th Infantry in Belleau and Givry. If Hill 193 should not be taken, the latter battalion,, in advancing up the shallow depression between Hills 193 and 190 against the stronghold of Les Brusses Farm, would be exposed, as also the battalion of the 103rd Infantry on its right, to enfilade fire from the left.

In the execution of the plan of attack the heavy guns of the division and corps failed absolutely to participate in the artillery preparation, and again the 167th French Division failed to take Hill 193. The left battalion (104th Infantry), attacking eastward on schedule time from Belleau, soon lost touch with the battalion on its right (103 rd Infantry), and after advancing a short distance with both flanks

French gun in action (front of Champagne)

exposed, dug in under a heavy fire. The 103rd Infantry also attacked on schedule time over the open ground in its front between Givry and Bouresches, but its left was soon held up by fire from Hill 193 and compelled to dig in, its right front and support companies alone reaching the objective on Hill 190. Holding on to the position they had won, they were reinforced during the night.

The obstacles which confronted the 51st Brigade on the right were less formidable than those encountered by the 52nd Brigade, and its attack was more successful than that of the latter. The chief difficulty in its path was caused by the fact that while the woods on its left front were apparently lightly held, its left regiment was facing east, and its right regiment north, so that without the most careful coordination of the attack there was grave danger of confusion and the intermingling of the assaulting battalions. However, the operation was well conducted.

The troops of the 102nd Infantry on the left promptly entered and cleared out the Bois de Bouresches in their front, while the 101st Infantry, echeloned to the left, and maintaining excellent liaison, established itself in the Bois de la Halmadière farther to the south. Upon the line indicated, progress ceased, as the brigade on the left had failed to advance, and the Germans still held a commanding position on Hill 204, east of Vaux, within the sector of the left division of the Thirty-ninth French Corps. This position for some time had successfully resisted the most serious efforts directed against it. In this situation the 26th U. S. Division rested on the night of July 20, during which the enemy effected a withdrawal from its front without molestation.

12: The Sixth Army, July 21st-24th

By the evening of July 20th, the Tenth and Sixth Armies had advanced the west face of the salient to the line of Berzy-le-Sec, Villem-ontoire, the outskirts of Le Plessier-Huleu, and Oulchy-la-Ville. From then on, the First U. S. Corps, with a front of seven kilometres held by the 26th U. S. and 167th French Divisions, which hitherto had been called on to advance nearly due east, was expected to swing gradually toward the northeast. Having been up to this time at the pivot of the operations directed against the plateau southwest of Soissons, its advance had necessarily depended upon the progress of the line on its left. But with the whole line straightened out by the forward movement of the corps on its left, the progress of the First Corps was no longer to be a mere following-up movement. With the Thirty-Eighth

French Corps on its right it was to make the greatest daily advance in conformity with the elements on its left. The enemy was to be pressed vigorously along a line swinging half to the left on a pivot resting on the Aisne, thus forcing him behind the Vesle.

Sometime during the night of the 19th the German High Command took the decision to effect a withdrawal on the night of the 20th. This decision was known at the headquarters of the First U. S. Corps during the afternoon of that day, so that orders were issued by 8 p.m. directing that an immediate pursuit be pressed. It was dawn of the 21st, however, before the leading elements of the 26th U. S. Division, in regimental columns, got under way. Early in the morning the 167th French Division occupied Hill 193, which cleared the way for an advance, but despite repeated urgings from Corps Headquarters the progress of the 26th U. S. Division was so slow that contact with the enemy was completely lost. It was 1 p.m. when the 52nd Brigade in the lead arrived at the Soissons-Château Thierry road, where, having reached the point designated as its objective for the day in the event strong resistance were encountered, it halted without thought of further pursuit, or of any attempt to regain contact with the retreating enemy, and proceeded to dig in.

At 4 p.m. the brigade commanders received an order which had taken twelve hours to reach them, directing them to resume the advance. They did so, but the division was no longer in condition to press, or even harry a resolute rear guard. During the late afternoon the leading unit of the left column, pushing eastward along the road leading to the villages of Trugny and Epieds, came into sudden contact with enemy machine guns, but when the battalion commander undertook to organise an attack upon the hostile position, he discovered that three of his companies had fallen back, leaving only the company forming his advance guard. Nor had the supporting battalion come up, as it had failed to receive the incompletely distributed order to press on at 4 o'clock. Under these circumstances the entire brigade again halted, this time for the night.

Like the 51st Brigade, the 52nd Brigade, advancing slowly in its subsector to the south, had completely lost contact with the enemy early in the morning. After halting on the Château Thierry road it too resumed its advance late in the afternoon, but upon discovering hostile machine guns in position near Trugny, the 102nd Infantry in advance withdrew to the woods on the east for the night, while the 101st Infantry went into bivouac a short distance in its rear.

Further delays in the distribution of orders made the success of a later attack very doubtful. Division Field Order No. 58, issued at 5:25 p.m., July 21st, urging "no delay or cessation" in the pursuit, did not reach Headquarters, 51st Brigade, until after midnight, and Headquarters, 52nd Brigade, until an even later hour, while the troops were resting in bivouac. Moreover, definite information as to the location of the front line never reached the artillery throughout the day of the projected advance. No wonder that virtually no progress was made.

An attack was delivered at daybreak on the 22nd by the 52nd Brigade, without artillery support. It was broken up, and the assaulting troops driven back to their original positions. It was reported that they had been fired upon by their own artillery during the initial stages of the attack. The 51st Brigade, attacking at 7:30 a.m., only succeeded in effecting a temporary lodgement in Trugny and Epieds, then, unsupported by artillery, it was driven from the positions it had gained. Two hours later the brigade delivered a second attack with an accompanying barrage, but the advance was checked with heavy loss on the open slopes west of Trugny. The 52nd Brigade, having made no further efforts to advance during the morning, made another unsuccessful attempt in the afternoon. Night fell with the whole line virtually unchanged.

The corps ordered an attack for 4:35 a.m. on the 23rd, and accordingly the 101st Infantry, which was comparatively fresh, was moved into the front line during the night. It was to be supported by the 101st Engineers. Despite the fact that the infantry assaulted after 7 a.m., two and a half hours late, after the artillery barrage had died down, the attack penetrated deeply into the Bois de Trugny, outflanking the villages of Epieds and Trugny, and bade fair at the outset to meet with great success. But, wholly unsupported by the artillery in the latter stages of its advance, it was finally checked at 10:15 a.m. The troops had made a splendid effort during the early morning. They were now subjected to a heavy fire from the left, and a prolonged bombardment with high explosive and gas shells, which compelled them to withdraw during the afternoon to their lines of the morning. There they were re-formed with commendable energy by the unit commanders preparatory to a new attack which was planned by the division, but which was later called off.

But the German plan of retreat had been upset. Though it had been determined on the 19th to commence the withdrawal to the Ourcq the following night, with the Vesle as the ultimate line of de-

Under the shells (Verdun)

fence so great was the pressure exerted by the Tenth French Army that the German High Command was compelled to throw its Ninth Army, under von Eben, into the line on the right of the Seventh Army to cover the withdrawal and to hold the positions in the region of Soissons. Thus during the succeeding days the Tenth Army was confronted by the Ninth German Army, while the entire Seventh German Army sought in vain to check the advance of the Sixth Army of the French.

Reinforcements had been urgently requested by the division commander of the 26th U. S. Division, on the night of the 22nd, and in compliance with his request the corps sent forward the 56th Brigade, 28th U. S. Division, placing it under his command. It was directed that this brigade take over the entire front line of the 26th Division, and attack at 4:05 a.m., July 24th. The night of the 23rd was spent in effecting the relief, which was accomplished only after great confusion and many irksome delays. It proved impossible, therefore, to launch the attack at the time ordered. The 167th French Division, however, did attack on time only to find that the enemy had retired.

During the 24th contact was again lacking between the 26th U. S. Division and the retreating enemy. The pursuit was taken up during the morning and proceeded to the Fère-Jaulgonne road, where the 26th Division was finally relieved on the night of the 24th of July by the 42nd U. S., the command within the sector passing at 7 a.m. on the 25th.

The casualties were at first reported as four thousand one hundred and eight, but it is certain that the permanent losses did not exceed two thousand. Only five hundred and ninety-five killed, and one thousand two hundred and forty-five seriously wounded, or a total of eighteen hundred and forty were subsequently reported. The division is credited with the capture of two hundred and forty prisoners during the entire week over which its operations extended.

While the 26th Division was following the enemy within the sector of the First U. S. Corps, the 3rd Division had taken up the pursuit of the enemy to the Ourcq. On the 19th, the Germans had succeeded in withdrawing from the southern bank of the river east of the 3rd Division almost without molestation. By the time a vigorous blow had been planned, and action taken to deliver it, it was too late, for when the attack was delivered, on the morning of the 20th, the enemy had already abandoned his lines, not only at the point of attack but north of the Marne as well. Working all day with unusual energy, though under the fire of hostile guns, the engineers succeeded in throwing across the Marne three floating bridges, in addition to a pontoon and a trestle bridge, over which the infantry crossed by the morning of the 21st. From the river the division pushed up the slopes on the north bank and across the high ground beyond, toward Le Charmel. Between the Forêt de Fère and the Forêt de Ris, which lay along the boundaries of its sector, progress was slow, for numerous machine gun nests had to be dealt with by the division during the 22nd, 23rd, and 24th. The fighting was at times severe at La Théodore and La Tienterne Farms on the left, and Les Franquets Farm on the great central ridge lying in the division sector.

Simultaneously with the relief of the 26th by the 42nd U. S. Division on the 25th of July, the 3rd was preparing to assault the town of Le Charmel, well to its right. But important developments in the Allied strategy, culminating on July 24th, must be outlined before an account is given of the progress of this attack.

13: The Opening of a New Phase

The 24th of July marks an important turning point in the affairs of the Allies. A glance at the appended chart disclosing the daily progress of the attack will show that on this date the line of the Tenth and Sixth Armies had swept forward to Buzancy on the left, Oulchy-le-Château in the centre, and to Le Charmel on the right. Although the Tenth Army had advanced after the 18th only with great difficulty and had made relatively slight daily gains, progress in the centre had been more rapid, owing to the withdrawal of the enemy to the Ourcq. So successful had the operation been as a whole that Marshal Foch determined to take the initiative and pass to a general offensive along the entire front of the Allies. With this object in view, a conference at his headquarters at Senlis was held on the 24th, attended by General Pershing and Sir Douglas Haig, where the general plan of operations was outlined.

Now, for the first time, a broad and comprehensive plan for the defeat of the enemy appears on the part of Marshal Foch. It is embodied in the memorandum, dealing with the military situation and the operations to be undertaken in the future, which he submitted to his subordinate commanders on July 24th, and upon which they agreed. The Allies had turned the 5th German offensive into a defeat for the enemy. They had at last reached an equality with, the enemy in the number of combatants, though not in the number of combat units.

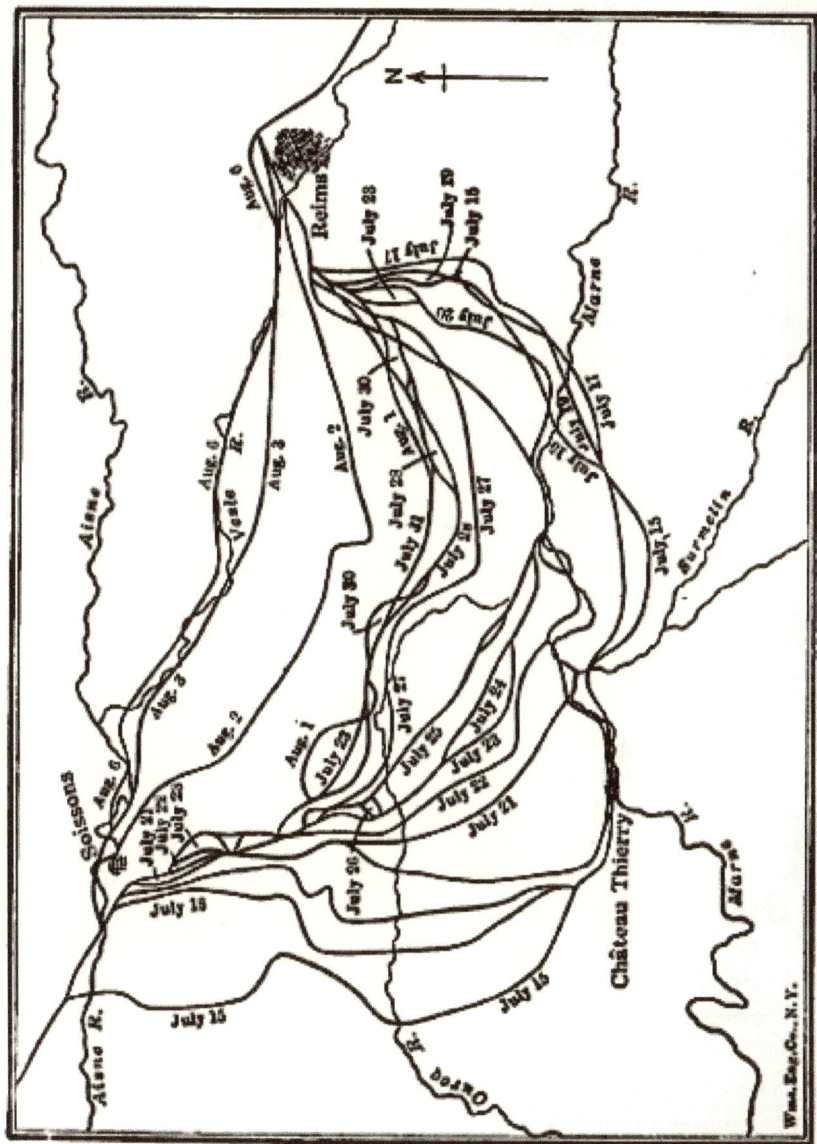

FROM THE MARNE
TO THE VESLE

For the first time they possessed a superiority in the number of their reserves. While the enemy was confronted with a grave and continuing crisis in maintaining the number of his effectives, two hundred and fifty thousand American reinforcements were arriving monthly for the Allies, who also possessed an unquestioned superiority of aviation and tank material, and already a small artillery superiority which would increase rapidly with the arrival of the American artillery.

Of the two armies which the enemy was compelled to maintain—one a holding army in the line, the other a shock army of manoeuvre at the disposal of the German High Command, the first was approaching exhaustion and the latter was much weakened. The Allies had taken the initiative in full combat, and their strength enabled them to retain it. Furthermore, the principles of war demanded that they do so. The moment had, in fact, come to abandon the general defensive attitude which had been imposed upon the Allies by numerical inferiority, and to pass to the offensive.

Though the 5th German offensive, which had already been turned into a defeat for the enemy, was first of all to be exploited by carrying on vigorous attacks without relaxation on the battlefield between the Aisne and the Marne, the consequences of these operations were to extend beyond this one battlefield. Certain operations preliminary to a decisive offensive were to be undertaken at once.

The first of these was to release the railroads indispensable to future operations. The minimum result of the present offensive was to be the release of the Paris-Avricourt railroad in the region of the Marne. The Paris-Amiens railroad was to be freed by the combined action of the British and French Armies. The Paris-Avricourt railroad in the region of Commercy was to be released by the reduction of the St. Mihiel salient, thus placing the Allies within striking distance of Briey and enabling them to operate, if necessary, on a large scale between the Meuse and the Moselle. The St. Mihiel operation was to be conducted by the American Army as soon as it was capable of performing such a task.

The second series of operations was to release the mining districts in the north, and to drive the enemy from the regions of Dunkirk and Calais. For this purpose two attacks were to be made, either separately or in conjunction, so planned as to hinder the enemy in the use of his reserves and to prevent their reconstitution. The attacks were to be powerfully prepared, and were to possess the element of surprise which the recent operations had shown to be indispensable to success.

No attempt was made by Marshal Foch to predict how far the operations outlined by him would carry the Allies into time and space. He declared, however, that it was advisable to plan in the present for an important offensive that might become possible for the late Summer or Autumn, the exact nature of which was not specified, though no doubt well understood. Finally, the marshal gave warning that the Germans would seek to avoid the pressure of the Allies and to save their effectives by withdrawing to shorter lines, as they had done after the great Somme battle of 1916. Such a manoeuvre was not to be permitted by the Allies, who were to watch the enemy closely and prevent leisurely withdrawals on his part.

So much for the views and plans of the Allied commander-in-chief on July 24th. They clearly indicate that American troops were to be held on the Marne and employed there as long as necessary in the operation in which they were then engaged. As early as July 10th, General Pershing, counting on newly arrived units, had agreed to relieve five divisions from sectors in the east of France during July and August, and to hold them subject to use elsewhere. On the 21st it had been agreed between him and Marshal Foch that two American groups should be formed, one to be employed in the Marne sector, the other to occupy the region of Nancy-Toul. Pursuant to this understanding, the 5th, 35th, and 28th U. S. Divisions were to be withdrawn from the front of the Seventh and transferred to the area of the Eighth French Army, on August 15th, 25th, and September 5th, respectively, while no more American divisions were to be assigned to the area of the former.

Accordingly on July 24th, the 1st American Army, with Headquarters at La Ferté-sous-Jouarre, was created, and two days later it was agreed that to this group should be assigned the 4th, 26th, 32nd, 42nd, 77th, and 82nd U. S. Divisions, while the Nancy-Toul group was to be composed of the 89th, 90th, and 92nd Divisions in the line, with the 1st, 2nd, 3rd, and 26th Divisions in reserve. The last four divisions, after being withdrawn from the Marne, were to be reconstituted as quickly as possible. From these facts it appears that the High Command did not intend to allow the projected St. Mihiel operation, or one in the region of the Meuse, to interfere with the present exploitation of the success on the Marne or with the continuance of American divisions in that region.

It is also important to note that the definite organisation of two American groups at this time marks the abandonment on the part of

135

GERMAN
PRISONERS

the French and British military authorities of all idea of absorbing the American combat units within their own organisations.[3] General Pershing, by unwavering persistence, had won a complete victory in the long struggle over this proposal, which had repeated itself again and again in various forms.

14: MORE AMERICANS

The 42nd U. S. Division, which took over the sector of the 26th U. S. Division on the morning of July 25th, came into the line comparatively fresh. Known as the "Rainbow Division" because it was composed of National Guard organisations from many States, it had been hastily organised and sent to France in October. After a period of gruelling training in the Rolampont area, near Langres, it had been sent into the line late in February in a quiet sector east of Lunéville for its first instruction in trench warfare. When the German offensive of March began, it was attached to the Twenty-first French Corps, and was stationed in a second line position on the front of the Fourth French Army east of Reims. It remained with this army until after the German Champagne Offensive of July 15th-18th had been defeated, and the enemy began to withdraw his troops from the front of the Fourth French Army. Then the division was ordered to entrain for the region northwest of Château Thierry, where it was to be at the disposal of the Sixth French Army.

After having withdrawn from the line on July 21st, the 84th Infantry Brigade had two days' rest near La Ferté-sous-Jouarre, then moved by trucks to the Forêt de Fère, where it relieved the 56th Brigade, 28th U. S. Division, at that time under the command of the 26th Division. Upon being relieved this brigade was posted in the Bois Jean Guillaume as division reserve. During the succeeding night the 83rd Brigade, 42nd Division, in accordance with Field Order No. 21, First U. S. Corps, relieved the 167th French Division, thus giving the 42nd U. S. Division the entire front of the First U. S. Corps.

The original front of the corps on July 18th was, perhaps, seven or more kilometres in width. The operations of July 20th had contracted the front considerably, and when the 26th U. S. Division was relieved its sector had dwindled to a trifle over two kilometres. The

---

3. The British now strenuously opposed the St. Mihiel operation on the ground that the American Army would either meet with unexpected success and be led too far for safety, or meet with a reverse which would impair its value in subsequent operations. In either event the psychological effect would be deleterious. They eventually abandoned their opposition.

combined front of the 167th and 164th French Divisions on its left was not much greater. The gradual narrowing of the division sectors was the logical consequence of the shortening of the front of the whole offensive as the salient was pressed in from the flanks and apex, and as the Allied line approached more nearly a straight line parallel to the Vesle. Thus, the battle line of the 18th between the Aisne and Jaulgonne, sixty-two kilometres in length, was reduced by July 26th to approximately forty-one kilometres along the Ourcq, and it contracted later to thirty-five kilometres along the Vesle, when it became stabilised. Consequently the attacking divisions tended to crowd together as they pressed northward, compelling the withdrawal of divisions from time to time and the constant redistribution of sectors. Especially rapid was the contraction north of Château Thierry at the apex of the receding salient.

The heavy fighting between the 18th and 25th, and the reinforcement of the enemy's line on the 22nd, had, despite the contraction of the entire front, compelled the use of more and more divisions in the front line and the relief of many divisions along the entire front. Thus, on the morning of the 25th, the Allied order of battle was as shown in the chart. North of the Ourcq, it had been necessary to place fifteen divisions in the front line, whereas the attack had been begun with but thirteen. However, the Sixth Army order of battle of the 25th was changed only as to the identity of the divisions in line, the number remaining the same. Confronting the seventeen French divisions of the Sixth French Army in the front line and in support were thirteen German divisions; eleven German divisions in the front line confronted twelve Allied divisions.

From July 25th on, it will be seen that the progress of the Allied line continued to be more rapid along the front of the Sixth than along that of the Tenth Army, which encountered energetic resistance. Along the front of the Sixth Army a withdrawal was being effected and a mere delaying action fought to cover it. But the enemy was determined to hold the line in the region of Soissons, as appears from his sudden and heavy reinforcement of his positions north of the Ourcq.

In the attack delivered by the 3rd U. S. Division on the morning of July 25th, the 4th Infantry, advancing along the ridge, and the 7th Infantry up the ravine to the east against Le Charmel, encountered serious resistance, and suffered heavy casualties, but reached their objective and consolidated the line gained during the night. For the afternoon of the 26th a new attack with an artillery preparation of two

XVIII
von Hutier

18 End of
June
10 RB ?

VII
von Boehn

5R July 1

IX
von Eben

EM XXVII CR
Laon

I
von Mudra

Soissons
Fère en
Tardenois

Staabs

XIII
Aisne

R.
Reims

Beginning
of July

117

128

Compiegne

Aisne R.

32U.S.

25

2.4.0C

XVC

XIVCR

XIVC

LBB

8 July
29
Veele

R.

X
Mangin

2U.S.

4U.S.

38

48

62

30C

19

34W

11C

168

131

163

4C

132

10DIC

124

Jaulgonne

26U.S.

60C

VI
Degoutte

1U.S.

66

Marne R.

28U.S.

73

Dormans

Marne R.

V
Berthelot

IV
Gouraud

Château-Thierry

IX
De Mitry

1CC

125

Wms. Eng. Co., N. Y.

OPPOSING ORDERS OF BATTLE, JULY 25, 1918

hours was planned by the Thirty-Eighth French Corps for the 3rd U. S. Division in concert with the 39th French Division on the left, but the assaulting battalions of the 3rd Division were hurled back as they tried to pass through Le Charmel, and the 39th French Division made no advance whatever. During the night the enemy resumed his withdrawal, so that on the 27th the 3rd Division advanced over five kilometres, taking the town of Ronchères and reaching the Ourcq itself on the 28th.

Opposite the First U. S. Corps, on the front taken over on July 25th by the 42nd U. S. Division, the Germans were at first inactive. Their positions between the Bois de Preaux were quiet on the morning of July 26th. But towards 2 p.m., they shelled the Bois de Beuvardes and the woods around La Logette Farm and north of Grande Marie Farm with phosgene gas, causing considerable loss to the Americans. At 4:50 p.m., under cover of a rolling barrage, the 84th Brigade attacked, entering the Forêt de Fère on the left, and taking La Croix Rouge Farm and the hostile position along the Jaulgonne-Fère-en-Tardenois road running into the Verte Jean Guillaume Woods, on the right. Meanwhile, touch was lost with the 39th French Division on the right, from the sector of which a heavy flanking fire was delivered upon the American line. The Brigade was compelled to withdraw after dark to the shelter of the Beuvardes Woods west of La Croix Rouge Farm, where the troops dug in for the night under a heavy bombardment.

In view of the strength of the German positions opposite the 42nd it was decided to make no effort to take them during daylight on the 27th, but to make a surprise attack that night. But first, the 83rd Brigade was to extend its left by taking over with one of its regiments the sector of the 164th French Division, thus giving to the 42nd U. S. Division a front of five kilometres. The attack was to be supported by the artillery of the 26th and. 42nd U. S., 164th and 167th French Divisions with a violent preparation lasting ten minutes, and powerful interdiction fire on the hostile strong-points. But at 1 p.m. on the 27th it was discovered that the enemy had fallen back upon the Ourcq toward Fismes, whereupon the pursuit was vigorously pressed through the Forêt de Fère to the open country northeast of it.

Prisoners captured during the 26th and 27th disclosed the fact that the 201st Division opposite the Americans had been reinforced by elements of two first-class shock divisions,—the 4th Guard and 28th Divisions,—and of the 10th Landwehr Division, and that serious resistance might be offered south of the Ourcq. But by 8 p.m. on the 27th . patrols and French armoured cars had reached the southern bank of the stream, while the 42nd U. S. Division had pressed northward in four columns to within one kilometre of its southern bank south of Sergy, taking over great quantities of abandoned material and stores.

A new American division entered the line on July 28th. Next to the 42nd Division was the 39th French Division on the left of the Thirty-Eighth French Corps, which had, from the beginning of the operations on the 15th, occupied the sector between the First U. S. Corps and the 3rd U. S. Division. Though tired, the 39th French Division in the advance of the Thirty-Eighth French Corps had taken the villages of Fresnes and Courmont, and on the night of the 27th-28th it held a line within one kilometre of the Ourcq itself, in prolongation of the front of the 42nd U. S. Division. On that night it was relieved by the 55th Brigade, 28th U. S. Division.

Of this division only the 56th Brigade, which on the night of July 23rd had relieved the 51st Brigade of the 26th U. S. Division, and joined in the pursuit of the enemy from Trugny to Beuvardes, had as yet been in action. The rest of the Division had remained wholly in support. The arrival of the Thirty-Eighth Corps on the Ourcq on the right of the First U. S. Corps, and the relief by the 28th U. S. Division of the 39th French Division on its left, resulted in the alignment of three American divisions—the 42nd, 28th, and 3rd—along a front from a point opposite Sergy to Ronchères inclusive.

During the advance of the First U. S. and Thirty-Eighth French Corps from the Marne to the Ourcq, each undoubtedly influenced to some extent the progress of the other. It is to be noted that within these corps sectors both the 42nd and 3rd U. S. Divisions had progressed more rapidly as a rule than the divisions on their flanks, and it is not, therefore, unreasonable to conclude that they had supplied that driving force which brought the First U. S. and Thirty-Eighth French Corps to the Ourcq in advance of the corps on their flanks.

Closely following the First U. S. Corps was the 4th U. S. Division, and behind it still another American division had appeared in the theatre of operations.

After its infantry units were withdrawn from the front line in the Second and Seventh French Corps, on July 19th and 22nd, the 4th U. S. Division was placed in reserve in the zone Marizy-Ste. Marie Bonnes-Hautevesnes-Brumetz-St. Quentin-Marizy-Ste. Geneviève. On July 24th the 7th Brigade was placed under the orders of the Sev-

GERMAN PRISONERS
AT SOUILLY

enth Corps, and during the night of the 24th-25th the 47th Infantry marched to the Bois du Châtelet and was assigned the task of cleaning up the wood, while the 39th Infantry, attached to the Second Corps, took up a position between La Croix and Rocourt. On July 25th the 58th Infantry was placed at the disposal of the 11th Corps, and that night took up a position west of Oulchy-la-Ville. There it remained until the night of the 2 6th-27th, when, moving forward to Brumetz, it rejoined its brigade.

The 32nd, the other American division, was composed of Michigan and Wisconsin National Guard organisations which had arrived in France late in February, and after the usual course of training, had been placed in a quiet sector of the line. Divided between the 53rd and 151st French Divisions, it had occupied a quiet sector in the Gap of Belfort, from which it was withdrawn between the 19th and 21st of July and transferred to the Marne. Detraining in the region of Verberie on the 24th and 25th, it was placed in reserve behind the First U. S. Corps on the 27th, with headquarters at Bethisy-St. Martin.

In the meantime the artillery brigades of the 4th and 28th U. S. Divisions had joined their units, so that before the advance reached the Ourcq there were in the Marne theatre of operations eight American divisions plus an artillery brigade attached to the First U. S. Corps, making a total of approximately two hundred thousand men. Of this number three divisions had been heavily engaged and may be said to have been unavailable for further offensive action.

15: THE BATTLE OF THE OURCQ

By July 28th, complete contact with the enemy had been regained along the Ourcq. A battle began on that day, named from the stream behind which the enemy chose to offer a new and more determined resistance to the advance of the Sixth Army while he was organising his ultimate line of resistance behind the Vesle.

Perceiving that the increasing resistance along the Ourcq was but to cover the ultimate withdrawal to the Vesle, and that the enemy would make a determined stand behind the latter stream, Marshal Foch decided that the proper hour was near for the launching of the British attack in the region of Amiens, which, as we have seen, he had outlined on the 24th of July, without setting any date for it. It was now ordered for August 8th. Concerning it the utmost secrecy was maintained, only three persons at Marshal Foch's headquarters knowing of the order. One copy was written out and taken to Sir Douglas Haig by

Marshal Foch's Chief of Staff on the 28th, and later another copy was delivered by a French Staff officer to General Debeney, commanding the First French Army, placing him under the British commander for the operation.

The 28th of July was a day of tremendous conflicts throughout the widely extended battle line that swept south-eastward from Soissons past Fère-en-Tardenois.

On the front of the Tenth Army all the crests to the west of the Crise were carried on the day of the attack. Hartennes-et-Taux and Grand Rozoy, farther to the south, were taken later, bringing the Soissons-Château. Thierry highway wholly within the Allied line, which had now advanced to within four kilometres of Soissons itself. On the front of the Sixth Army the main conflict occurred along the Ourcq east of Fère-en-Tardenois between Sergy and Ronchères. There the First U. S. Corps and the two American divisions of the Thirty-Eighth French Corps on its right assailed positions of extraordinary natural strength, which presented by far the most serious obstacle yet encountered by the Americans on the front of the Sixth Army.

This, indeed, was a battlefield never to be forgotten. Of truly grand proportions, lying within a region of surpassing beauty, it was a fitting arena for the bitter struggle that was to ensue throughout days of blue sky and soft sunshine. From Ronchères on the south, the Ourcq follows a north-westerly course past Sergy on its north bank to Fère-en-Tardenois, where it turns abruptly to the west and loses itself to view. For a distance of ten kilometres the stream, and the verdant valley through which it courses, are visible from the hills which skirt its southern bank.

Opposite, like bastions in the great wall of hills, stand Côte 212, rising to a height of seventy meters above the stream half a mile or more southeast of Sergy, and Côte 184 on the left of the town, while from these summits the hills range away to the north and south, sloping down to an elevation of twenty meters above the stream at Sergy itself. Dense thickets clothe the hillsides, or screen the innumerable ravines that scar them, affording excellent cover for defenders from the view and fire of assailants, while on the reverse slopes of the hills the number of positions for hostile guns is unlimited. From Côte 212 and the adjacent summits, one can obtain the most complete observation over all approaches to the stream.

The Ourcq had been swollen by the rains of early July to a width of fifteen and a depth of three meters. Both bridges near Sergy had

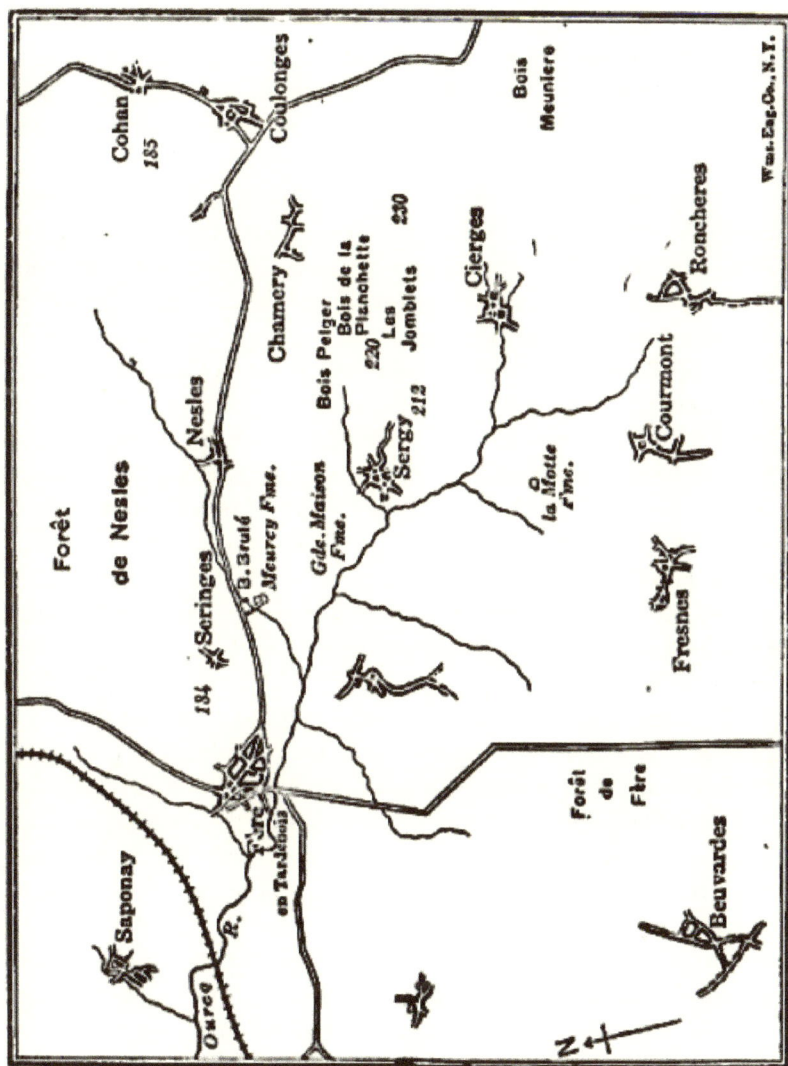

THE OURCQ
BATTLEFIELD

been destroyed. Every crossing was overlooked by the high ground along its steep north bank, the forbidding position upon which the enemy was found in reinforced strength by the three American divisions. Opposed to the 42nd U. S. Division alone, from right to left the enemy had in line the 201st, 4th Guard, 6th Bavarian, and 10th Landwehr Reserve, and in the course of the next four days the 1st Guard, 5th Guard, and 17th Divisions, and a battalion of the 216th Division, were thrown into the line.

While the 28th and 3rd U. S. Divisions on its right were attempting to force a crossing of the Ourcq on the front of the Thirty-Eighth Corps, the 42nd U. S. Division advanced to the stream on the front of the First U. S. Corps in line of regiments in column of battalions, with the 84th and 85th Brigades on the right and left, respectively. As the troops commenced the descent of the slopes on the southern bank they were met with heavy rifle and machine gun fire from the hills around Meusey Farm and Sergy. Though they were thrown back at first, by 10:30 a.m. elements of all four regiments succeeded in crossing the river by fords that were soon discovered near the town. These parties at once came under the fire of hostile guns, posted on the edge of the Forêt de Nesles and very accurately adjusted with the aid of planes. The divisional artillery, with its guns posted well back from the river behind the ridge at L'Espérance Farm and La Four-à-Verre, was unable to suppress this annoying fire.

The capture of positions in the outskirts of Sergy by the 84th Brigade on the left failed to relieve the situation, only serving to bring the line under the enfilading fire of machine guns in the small thickets of Pelger, De la Planchette, and Les Jomblets, on the crest of Côte 212. These machine guns caused the utmost embarrassment. In this situation the division was vigorously counterattacked by the 4th Guard Division, one of the best shock divisions of the German Army, which had been brought into close support the night preceding. The counter-attack succeeded in ejecting the American troops from the outskirts of Sergy, but they rallied at the river bank, and, returning to the attack, again established themselves in the western edge of the town. Their position here was alternately occupied by opposing patrols no less than three times during the day, but remained in the hands of the Americans from 8 p.m. throughout the night.

The town itself was repeatedly visited by small parties of both sides, but does not appear to have been actually possessed by either the Germans or Americans during this period. After a bombardment which continued intermittently through the night, a second counter-attack by the 4th Guard Division was delivered upon the 84th Brigade in the morning, which again drove the Americans away from the immediate vicinity of Sergy.

The 28th U. S. Division, which had been returned to the control of the Thirty-Eighth French Corps on the 26th, was to have effected the relief of the 39th French Division during the night of July 27th-28th in front of Cierges and the Bois des Grimpettes. It was to push across the stream immediately, but its advance had been greatly delayed by the failure of the French guides to appear for the relief. The sun was up, therefore, on the 28th before the 55th Brigade had fully taken over the sector. It then advanced on a front of two battalions. But stout resistance from La Motte Farm on the left prevented, until 3 p.m., the bridging of the swollen stream and the crossing of the leading elements of the brigade.

Immediately after the crossing a raking fire from Hill 212 and the woods to the north and east caused the front line to dig in about five hundred meters north of the river bank. Here it was further subjected to an embarrassing fire from the woods north of Ronchères in the sector of the 3rd U. S. Division, which, attacking on July 28th with but one regiment—4th Infantry—on the right of the 28th, had crossed the stream and taken Ronchères in the face of no very great resistance.

That night a general attack was prepared, to be delivered on the following morning by the whole 42nd Division. The 84th Brigade on the right again moved against Sergy, and the 83rd Brigade on the left against Meurcy Farm and Seringes-et-Nesles. By noon Sergy was taken, and later Meurcy Farm, Côte 184, and finally Seringes. Darkness on July 29th found the front line of the 42nd established in these positions, after a day of fighting which may be styled desperate.

The resistance encountered by the 3rd Division on the 29th was sufficient to check its progress completely. The Bois Meunière north of the stream beyond Ronchères was strongly held, and the attacking battalion, which advanced at 3:40 p.m. with both flanks unprotected, was roughly handled. Evidently there was increasingly stubborn resistance ahead and the division was exhausted. Accordingly, its relief by the 32nd U. S. Division commenced that night, and the following day it withdrew from the front line.

During the 29th, the 4th U. S. Division, which had come under the control of the 1st U. S. Corps the preceding day, was assembled in the

Bois de Châtelet in close support of the 42nd. Two battalions of the 47th Infantry were attached to the 42nd which were engaged with the 84th Brigade in the fighting of the next day.

All during the night of the 29th, the German machine gun and artillery fire continued without intermission, the latter heavier than the day before. It was evident that the Americans held their existing line by a precarious tenure, so long as the three small woodlands on Côte 212, the crest of Côte 163, between Seringes and Nesles, and the Forêt de Nesles, opposite the 42nd Division, remained in the enemy's hands.

Therefore, at 9 o'clock on the morning of the 30th, the 168th Infantry advanced toward Nesles and the 167th and 165th on its left toward the *château* and woods of Nesles, while the 166th Infantry held Seringes and Côte 184. Terrific enfilade and frontal machine gun fire at once met them, as well as increased artillery bombardment. But the excellent marksmanship of the American batteries, particularly those of the 101st Field Artillery, which were supporting it, enabled the 167th Infantry to realize substantial progress. Part of the success of the day is to be attributed to good liaison between the infantry and artillery.

By noon on July 30th, the 167th Infantry crossed the wooded plateau of Nesles and established itself in a hollow protected from machine gun fire. But, unfortunately, the 168th, on the right, and the 165th, on the left, had been unable to make similar progress. The former regiment, after pushing for about five hundred meters up the slope of the hill northeast of Sergy, was stopped by machine guns along the crest and in the woods on Côte 212, and compelled to dig in. The 165th could not progress out of the deep hollow on the Ru du Pont Brulé because of the machine guns in the small Bois Brulé a few hundred metres up the creek, and those farther back, in the Forêt de Nesles. Thus both flanks of the 167th were exposed in its new position.

The 166th Infantry, in Seringes and on Côte 184, did not attempt to advance during the day. In the afternoon the enemy counter-attacked the village by gradual infiltration, which the Americans allowed to proceed until after dark. When a good many troops had entered the town it was suddenly surrounded and completely cleared of the enemy. A German counterattack, late in the afternoon, on Côte 184, was also repulsed. But the day's actual progress was very slight, and was gained at the cost of extremely fierce fighting and heavy losses. The division surgeon reported the wounded from July 24th up to 8 a.m., July 30th, as three thousand two hundred and seventy-five, of whom eighty-nine *per cent*, however, were cleared as slightly wounded.

The 3rd Division, having been relieved during the night of July 29th-30th, the 28th and 32nd U. S. Divisions made a joint attack, preceded by an artillery preparation of thirty minutes, on the morning of the 30th. The attack broke down, and was repeated at 9 a.m. with no better success. From the Bois des Grimpettes, and from the sector on its right in which the 4th French Division of the Third Corps failed to advance, a withering enfilade fire checked all progress on the part of the 32nd Division, while the fire from the north and the village of Cierges held up the 28th Division on its left. At 2:30 p.m., under cover of a rolling barrage, the two divisions again advanced, the 28th Division reaching the outskirts of Cierges, and the 32nd Division clearing out the Bois des Grimpettes. The 28th Division, though engaged only briefly in the front line, was exhausted by two weeks of constant exposure, and was relieved that night by the 63rd Brigade, 32nd U. S. Division, which took over its sector, the command passing at 9 a.m., July 31st. It was then moved back into support, and stationed on a secondary line in the Argentel Ravine, and on Hill 224 east of Château Charmel.

On July 31st, the administrative command hitherto exercised by the First U. S. Corps over the 3rd, 28th, and 32nd U. S. Divisions was transferred to the Third U. S. Corps, from which the 1st and 2nd U. S. were transferred to the Fourth U. S. Corps, with headquarters at Neufchâteau. The 1st Corps henceforth was composed of the 4th, 26th, and 42nd Divisions, over which it exercised complete control, whereas the three divisions of the Third Corps remained under the tactical command of the Thirty-Eighth French Corps. During the afternoon the 32nd Division attacked Les Jomblets with magnificent *élan*, clearing out the machine gun nests that had held up the 28th Division. But though the 64th Brigade on the right took Cierges at 2 p.m., the 63rd Brigade was driven back on the left.

To return to the 42nd Division, the elements of the 47th Infantry which had been attached to the 84th Brigade on the 29th were relieved on July 31st by the 39th Infantry, 4th U. S. Division. The situation along the front of the division remained almost a deadlock during the day, except on the right. Though carried on as vigorously as on the day preceding, the fighting of the 31st produced few changes except that the men of the 165th Infantry, who were in the constantly shelled ruins of Meurcy Farm, fell a few hundred meters back from it into the small Bois Colas. Along the rest of the line the troops dug in, except on the extreme right, where the 168th took a part of the Bois les Jomblets, the southern portion of Bois de la Planchette, and the highest part of the upland between them, called Côte 220.

The necessity here experienced of gaining ground inch by inch with the utmost caution caused the publication of an interesting memorandum at the advance divisional command post at 1 p.m., in which it was directed that within spheres of enemy artillery and machine gun resistance the normal attack formation in waves should not be adopted. Small patrols of ten to fifteen men were to move forward in scout fashion, crawling and utilising all depressions in the terrain, while the main body, halting under cover, was to assist their advance by the fire of Stokes mortars and 37 mm. guns. Batteries of 75 mm. guns were to be run up to the line when direct fire against enemy nests was practicable.

Though the diminution of the German aerial activity and artillery fire in the afternoon and numerous retrograde movements observed behind the enemy's lines indicated that he was making preparations to withdraw, he held his positions tenaciously throughout the following night and the day of August I St. Indeed, during that day both artillery fire and aerial activity increased, and though the 42nd U. S. Division captured Bois Brulé, a German infantry attack slightly forced back parts of its front. During the night of August 1st-2nd, the 4th U. S. Division commenced the relief of the 42nd in the Forêt de Fère. So ended the Battle of the Ourcq. From July 26th to August 1st, the First U. S. Corps had been held up along the river, and had not dislodged the enemy from his position.

16: The Battle of the Vesle

While he was holding the First U. S. Corps in check on the Ourcq from July 26th to August 1st, the enemy also fought to a complete standstill the Second French Corps on the left and the Thirty-Eighth Corps on the right. Only his withdrawal now enabled them to progress. During the period of the battle the First U. S. Corps had occupied a salient position in the line of the Sixth Army, in advance of the corps on its flanks. On August 1st the line was rectified, and the following day progress toward the Vesle was resumed along the whole front in the face of slight resistance. That night the line of the Tenth and Sixth Armies lay from Soissons in an almost due easterly direction toward Reims.

Shortly after daybreak on August 2nd, the 42nd U. S. Division, whose relief was not completed, advanced toward the north, meeting along its line only occasional bursts of machine gun and long-range artillery fire. By evening the front lay roughly east and west north of Les Bons Hommes Farm, representing an average advance within the corps of three kilometres. That same day, after a brief artillery preparation, the 32nd U. S. Division, now covering the entire front of the Thirty-Eighth French Corps, advanced at 4:45 a.m., end also met with little resistance. It passed on through Chamery to Dravegny, a distance of six kilometres. Resuming its progress on August 3rd, it advanced seven kilometres, its left finally resting one kilometre south of the Vesle and its right two kilometres south of Fismes, where heavy resistance developed.

At dawn on the 3rd of August, the advance elements of the 42nd U. S. Division entered Chéry-Châtreuse. During the morning its relief by the 4th U. S. Division was completed, and it was withdrawn to the Forêt de Fère in support, while the 4th took over the front line in the entire First U. S. Corps sector. It was disposed with the 8th Brigade on the right and the 7th on the left, the front line running east and west through the Forêt de Nesles. During the day it advanced to the heights south of the Vesle without opposition, establishing its line along Hills 204-208-210.

Upon reaching the Vesle on the 3rd, the First U. S. Corps took over the sector of the Second French Corps on its left, assuming command in the transfer of the 62nd French Division. On August 4th, therefore, the First U. S. Corps, with the 62nd French and 4th U. S. Divisions in the front line, and the 42nd U. S. Division in support; the Thirty-Eighth French Corps with the 32nd U. S. Division in the front line and the 28th U. S. Division in support; and the Third French Corps, with the 4th French Division in the front line and the 18th French Division in support, formed a continuous line from east to west along the southern bank of the Vesle, thus having completed the original task set for the Sixth Army. The next day Soissons was entered by the French Cavalry of the Tenth Army on its left. The fight which ensued was carried on in an effort to determine definitely the positions of the new German main line of resistance. With that purpose in view a general advance across the Vesle was ordered.

On August 4th the entire line moved forward to the Vesle, but was promptly met by intense artillery and machine gun fire which checked all progress. Patrols succeeded in crossing the river on the 5th, but that night they were withdrawn to permit an artillery preparation for a general attack. At 4:30 a.m. on the 6th, the infantry advanced under cover of a rolling barrage. In the sector of the First U. S. Corps, the 8th Brigade of the 4th U. S. Division on the right gained the Soissons-Reims road, but the 7th Brigade on the left failed to cross the river. During the night of August 6th-7th, the 28th U. S. Division relieved the 32nd in the front line of the Thirty-Eighth French Corps.

Officially the Aisne-Marne Offensive ended on August 6th. The line as established by the enemy north of the Vesle during the first days of the month was that upon which the offensive may be said to have terminated. Along that line the situation eventually became stabilised, and active operations ceased after the enemy's main line of resistance had been fully developed. However, very severe fighting in continuation of the preceding operations continued for several days longer-in the general effort to cross the Vesle. On the morning of the 7th, the 4th U. S. Division again attacked and succeeded in entering Bazoches, but the 62nd French Division on its left failed to advance and the 4th U. S. Division was driven back by a counter-attack, first to the railroad south of the town, and finally about 7:30 p.m. to the south bank of the Vesle.

Such was the situation on the Vesle when the Somme Offensive of the Allies was launched on August 8th. During the preceding ten days the preparations for the offensive on the Amiens front had been completed by Sir Douglas Haig and General Debeney with such secrecy that British prisoners taken by the Germans two days before it began were quite ignorant that an attack was contemplated.

But the action of the British on the Somme did not alter the determination of the enemy to hold the positions he had organised behind the Vesle, which he clung to with the utmost tenacity. On August 10th the 8th Brigade, 4th U. S. Division, succeeded in taking Château Diable and cleaning out the surrounding woods. Its line remained established along the railroad between the Vesle and the Reims road on the right, and the railroad on the south bank of the Vesle on the left. In that position the First U. S. Corps was finally relieved on the night of August 11th-12th, by the 77th U. S. Division, Third U. S. Corps, whereupon the 4th, less artillery, withdrew to the Bois de Dole and the Forêt de Nesles, marching to the Forêt de Fère the following night.

During its operations the 4th Division lost two hundred and ten officers and five thousand nine hundred and forty-four men, of which number thirty-eight officers and seven hundred and fourteen men were killed, the total losses being six thousand one hundred and fifty-four. In the 32nd Division the losses during the three days of August 4th, 5th, and 6th were reported as two thousand officers and men killed and wounded. These figures are indicative of the nature of the resistance encountered by the American troops on the Vesle. On August 13th, the headquarters of the First U. S. Corps were re-established at La Ferté-sous-Jouarre, the corps having been in line thirty-nine days.

During the twenty days over which its operations in the Aisne-Marne Offensive extended, the 26th, 42nd, and 4th U. S. Divisions, under its command, had taken six hundred and seventy-four prisoners from twelve German divisions. The Third U. S. Corps, composed of the 3rd, 26th, 28th, and 77th Divisions, with the last two remaining in the line, was now to hold the line to which the Americans had fought their way from the Marne.

17: THE AMERICAN CONTRIBUTION

What shall be our conclusions as to the part performed by American troops in the Aisne-Marne Offensive? Even without considering the moral effect of their presence, we have found that the influence of their actual fighting was marked. Viewed as a bulge in the hostile line, the Marne salient was from the first compressed on the fronts both of the Tenth Army on its western face, and of the Sixth Army on the south, exactly in accordance with the advance of the Third and First U. S. Corps, retracting at no point faster than the progress of the American divisions. On no day did the fighting end with the American units less far advanced than the French units on their flanks, and throughout the operations American troops were found occupying salient positions in the general line. Such salients were marked in the case of the divisions of the Third U. S. Corps attached to the Twentieth French Corps southwest of Soissons, and in the case of the First U. S. Corps in its advance to the Ourcq and the Vesle. Whatever else may be said, it is an indisputable fact that the American troops generally arrived at their successive objectives in the lead.[4]

---

4. This fact would be significant of the comparative pressure exerted upon the enemy's line by the American and French units, and of their fighting efficiency and effectiveness, if it were not for the fact that the American divisions, though charged with no greater frontage, possessed double the numerical strength of the French and an auxiliary armament of far greater fire-power.

No further comparison between the American and French combat units engaged side by side in the Aisne-Marne Offensive will here be attempted. But at this point it is desirable to call attention to certain differences between the American divisions themselves that operated on the Marne in July, 1918—differences more in the general characteristics of the units than in the actual tactical methods employed by them. Intangible as they may seem, these differences existed among combat divisions throughout the American Expeditionary Forces in France, owing to the varied influences of their preparatory training.

In the American Army there were found some divisions with highly developed French, and some with highly developed British characteristics. There were others which, by reason of long service under a more or less independent divisional command, developed purely American characteristics. Of the last order, the 1st and 2nd Divisions are examples, and of the French order the 26th and 42nd Divisions may be taken as variant types. The divisions which developed British characteristics were engaged at a later period than that with which we are dealing, so that we are not concerned with them here.

The principal distinction between the two orders mentioned was to be found in the impetuosity or headlong nature of the infantry attack. Neither order appeared to display more resolution than the other, but one was more characteristically American in its dash and seemed to possess a driving power which carried it along even in the face of intense opposition, despite the greater losses which such tactics probably entailed.

It is difficult to arrive at a general conclusion as to which of the two methods, systems, or orders was the better. To the French, after the terrible experiences at Morhange and elsewhere at the outbreak of the war, after the example of the British losses due to impetuosity, and the great drain on French manpower over four years of warfare, the French method was undoubtedly well adapted. It was without question the better under some circumstances. Certain it is that in the pursuit of an enemy as skilled as the Germans in covering their withdrawal with a deep screen of machine guns supported by artillery, the more deliberate development of the opposition minimizes losses and in the end, perhaps, involves little delay. On the other hand, when the enemy position is once developed, it is not always possible at the proper moment to abandon the slower method in favour of a violent push.

The comparative efficiency of the American and French staffs is not to be discussed here. But it should be stated that the blunders of the Americans were inevitable under the circumstances. The friction with which the American military mechanism operated was far less than might reasonably have been expected of it in view of its newness and the dual control exercised over it. What was accomplished in the way of actual fighting by American troops could, no doubt, have been done by other and more experienced troops if the Allies had had them available for use. The assertion may perhaps be challenged that the American troops carried out their missions with greater energy and power than those with whom they were associated. But there is one fact that cannot be disputed with reason, namely, that it was the presence of American troops on the Marne which made the success of the offensive of July 18th possible.

One need only recur to the statements of the Allied commander-in-chief at the conference of July 24th:

At last we have reached a numerical superiority over the enemy m the actual number of combatants.

For the first time the reserves of the Allies are superior to those of the enemy.

We are arriving at the turning of the road.

We have taken the offensive in full combat, and having taken the initiative must retain it.

The enemy is confronted with a grave crisis in maintaining his effectives, while monthly two hundred and fifty thousand American reinforcements for the Allies are arriving.

Our slight superiority in artillery will rapidly enhance with the coming of the American artillery into action.

These and other declarations by Marshal Foch are too plain to leave any doubt as to the influence which the actual presence of our two hundred and fifty thousand combatant troops bore upon his original decision to assume the offensive. Nor is it unreasonable to conclude that those troops tipped the scales of victory.

Appendices

APPENDIX I

ORGANIZATION 1st U. S. DIVISION

June 22, 1918

Major-General Robert L. Bullard, Commanding.
Lieutenant-Colonel Campbell King, Chief of Staff.
Lieutenant-Colonel G. K. Wilson, Asst. Chief of Staff, G-1.
Major W. C. Sherman, Asst. Chief of Staff, G-2.
Lieutenant-Colonel Geo. C. Marshall, Asst. Chief of Staff, G-3.

1ST INFANTRY BRIGADE
    Brigadier-General John L. Hines, Commanding.
    16th Regiment Infantry, Colonel F. E. Bamford.
    18th Regiment Infantry, Colonel Frank Parker.
    2nd Machine Gun Battalion, Major L. E. Hohl.

2ND INFANTRY BRIGADE
    Brigadier-General Beaumont B. Buck, Commanding.
    26th Regiment Infantry, Colonel Hamilton Smith.
    28th Regiment Infantry, Colonel Hanson E. Ely.
    3rd Machine Gun Battalion, Major C. A. Davis.

1ST FIELD ARTILLERY BRIGADE
    Brigadier-General C. P. Summerall, Commanding.

5th Regiment F.A., Lieutenant-Colonel Maxwell Murray.

6th Regiment F.A., Lieutenant-Colonel Cortlandt Parker.

7th Regiment F.A., Colonel L. T. Holbrook.

1st Machine Gun Battalion, Lieutenant-Colonel F. S. Bowen.

1st Regiment Engineers, Colonel L. V. Frasier.

2nd Field Signal Battalion, Major R. B. Paddock.

Trains, Colonel F. G. Lawton.

APPENDIX II

TABLE OF ORGANIZATION OF AMERICAN FORCES ENGAGED IN THE AISNE-MARNE OFFENSIVE (SECOND BATTLE OF THE MARNE)

July 18–August 6, 1918

FIRST U. S. CORPS

Major-General Hunter Liggett, Commanding.

Brigadier-General Malin Craig, Chief of Staff.

(3rd, 4th, 26th, 28th, 32nd, and 42nd U. S. Divisions)

3RD U. S. DIVISION (Regular)

Major-General Joseph T. Dickman, Commanding.

Colonel Robert H. C. Kelton, Chief of Staff.

5th Infantry Brigade—Brigadier-General Fred W. Sladen.

(4th Infantry, 7th Infantry, 8th Machine Gun Battalion).

6th Infantry Brigade—Brigadier-General Charles Crawford.

(30th Infantry, 38th Infantry, 9th Machine Gun Battalion).

3rd Field Artillery Brigade—Brigadier-General Wm. M. Cruikshank.

(10th and 76th Field Artillery [75 mm. guns]),

(18th Field Artillery [155 mm. howitzers]),

(3rd Trench Mortar Battery).

Special Troops—

7th Machine Gun Battalion, 6th Regiment Engineers, 5th Field Signal Battalion.

4TH U. S. DIVISION (Regular)

Major-General George H. Cameron, Commanding.

Lieutenant-Colonel Christian A. Bach, Chief of Staff.

7th Infantry Brigade—Brigadier-General Benjamin A. Poore.

(39th Infantry, 4th Infantry, 11th Machine Gun Battalion).

8th Infantry Brigade—Brigadier-General Frank D. Webster.

(58th Infantry, 59th Infantry, 12th Machine Gun Battalion).

4th Field Artillery Brigade—Brigadier-General Edwin B. Babbitt.

(16th and 77th Field Artillery [75 mm. guns]),

(13th Field Artillery [155 mm. howitzers]),

(4th Trench Mortar Battery).

Special Troops—

10th Machine Gun Battalion, 4th Regiment Engineers, 8th Field Signal Battalion.

26TH U. S. DIVISION (New England National Guard)

Major-General Clarence R. Edwards, Commanding.

Lieutenant-Colonel Duncan K. Major, Chief of Staff.

51st Infantry Brigade—Brigadier-General George H. Shelton.

(101st Infantry, 102nd Infantry, 102nd Machine Gun Battalion).

52nd Infantry Brigade—Brigadier-General Charles H. Cole.

(103rd Infantry, 104th Infantry, 103rd Machine Gun Battalion).

51st Field Artillery Brigade—Brigadier-General Dwight B. Aultman.

(101st and 102nd Field Artillery [75 mm. guns]),

(103rd Field Artillery [155 mm. howitzers]),

(101st Trench Mortar Battery).

Special Troops—

101st Machine Gun Battalion, 101st Regiment Engineers,

101st Field Signal Battalion.

28TH U. S. DIVISION (Pennsylvania National Guard) Major-General Charles H. Muir, Commanding.

Brigadier-General Edward L. King, Acting Chief of Staff.

55th Infantry Brigade—Brigadier-General Thomas W. Darrah.

(109th Infantry, 110th Infantry, 108th Machine Gun Battalion).

56th Infantry Brigade—Brigadier-General William Weigel.

(111th Infantry, 112th Infantry, 109th Machine Gun Battalion).

53rd Field Artillery Brigade—Brigadier-General William G. Price.

(107th and 109th Field Artillery [75 mm. guns]),

(108th Field Artillery [155 mm. howitzers]),

159

(103rd Trench Mortar Battery).

Special Troops—

107th Machine Gun Battalion, 103rd Regiment Engineers, 103rd Field Signal Battalion.

32ND U. S. DIVISION (Michigan and Wisconsin National Guard)

Major-General William G. Haan, Commanding.

Lieutenant-Colonel Robert McC. Beck, Acting Chief of Staff.

63rd Infantry Brigade—Brigadier-General William D. Connor.

(125th Infantry, 126th Infantry, 120th Machine Gun Battalion).

64th Infantry Brigade—Brigadier-General E. B. Winans.

(127th Infantry, 128th Infantry, 121st Machine Gun Battalion).

66th Field Artillery Brigade—Brigadier-General William Lassiter.

(147th and 148th Field Artillery [75 mm. guns]),

(146th Field Artillery [155 mm. howitzers]),

(116th Trench Mortar Battery).

Special Troops—

119 Machine Gun Battalion, 107th Engineers, 107th Field Signal Battalion.

42ND U. S. DIVISION (Mixed National Guard)

Major-General Charles T. Menoher, Commanding.

Brigadier-General Douglas MacArthur, Chief of Staff.

83rd Infantry Brigade—Brigadier-General Michael J. Lanihan.

(165th Infantry, 166th Infantry, 150th Machine Gun Battalion).

84th Infantry Brigade—Brigadier-General Robert A. Brown.

(167th Infantry, 168th Infantry, 151st Machine Gun Battalion).

67th Field Artillery Brigade—Brigadier-General George G. Gatley.

(149th and 161st Field Artillery [75 mm. guns]),

(150th Field Artillery [155 mm. howitzers]),

(117th Trench Mortar Battery).

Special Troops—

149th Machine Gun Battalion, 117th Engineers, 117th Field Signal Battalion.

THIRD U. S. CORPS

Major-General Robert Lee Bullard, Commanding.

Brigadier-General Alfred W. Bjornstad, Chief of Staff.

1ST U. S. DIVISION (Regular)

Major-General Charles P. Summerall, Commanding.

Colonel Campbell King, Chief of Staff.

1st Infantry Brigade—Brigadier-General John L. Hines.

(16th Infantry, 18th Infantry, 2nd Machine Gun Battalion).

2nd Infantry Brigade—Brigadier-General Beaumont B. Buck.

(26th Infantry, 28th Infantry, 3rd Machine Gun Battalion).

1st Field Artillery Brigade—Colonel L. T. Holbrook.

(5th and 6th Field Artillery [75 mm. guns]),

(7th Field Artillery [155 mm. howitzers]),

(1st Trench Mortar Battery).

Special Troops—

    1st Machine Gun Battalion, 1st Regiment Engineers, 2nd Field Signal Battalion.

2ND U. S. DIVISION (Regular)

Major-General James G. Harbord, Commanding.
Colonel Preston Brown, Chief of Staff.

3rd Infantry Brigade—Brigadier-General Hanson E. Ely.

    (9th Infantry, 23rd Infantry, 5th Machine Gun Battalion).

4th Infantry Brigade—Brigadier-General John A. Lejeune.

    (5th Marines, 6th Marines, 6th Machine Gun Battalion).

2nd Field Artillery Brigade—Brigadier-General A. J. Bowley.

    (12th and 15th Field Artillery [75 mm. guns]),

    (17th Field Artillery [155 mm. guns]),

    (2nd Trench Mortar Battery).

Special Troops—

    4th Machine Gun Battalion, 2nd Regiment Engineers, 1st Field Signal Battalion.

When the Tide Turned

By Otto H. Kahn

An Address at the United War Work Campaign Meeting of the
Boston Athletic Association November 12, 1918

Why the Tide Was Fated to Turn

These are soul-stirring days. To live through them is a glory and a
solemn joy. The words of the poet resound in our hearts: "God's in His
heaven, all's well with the world."

Events have shaped themselves in accordance with the eternal law.
Once again the fundamental lesson of all history is borne in upon the
world, that evil—though it may seem to triumph for a while—carries
within it the seed of its own dissolution. Once again it is revealed
to us that the God-inspired soul of man is unconquerable and that
the power, however formidable, which challenges it is doomed to go
down in defeat.

A righteous cause will not only stand unshaken through trials and
discomfiture, but it will draw strength from the very set-backs which
it may suffer. A wrongful cause can only stand as long as it is buoyed
up by success.

The German people were sustained by a sheer obsession akin to
the old-time belief in the potent spell of "the black arts" that their
military masters were invulnerable and invincible, that by some power—good or evil, they did not care which—they had been made so,
and that the world was bound to fall before them.

The nation was immensely strong only as long as that obsession
remained unshaken. With its destruction by a series of defeats which
were incapable of being explained as "strategic retreats," their morale
crumbled and finally collapsed, because it was not sustained, as that of
the Allies was sustained in the darkest days of the war by the faith that

they were fighting for all that men hold most sacred.

To those who were acquainted with German mentality and psychology, it had been manifest all along that when the end foreordained did come, it would come with catastrophic suddenness.

WHERE THE TIDE TURNED

It is the general impression that the tide of victory set in with Marshal Foch's splendid movement against the German flank on July 18th. That movement, it is true, started the irresistible sweep of the wave which was destined to engulf and destroy the hideous power of Prussianism. But the tide which gathered and drove forward the waters out of which that wave arose, had turned before. It turned with and through the supreme valour of our Marines and other American troops in the *first* battle at Château Thierry and at Belleau Wood, *in the first week of June.*

The American force engaged was small, measured by the standard of numbers to which we have become accustomed in this war, but the story of their fighting will remain immortal and in its psychological and strategic consequences the action will take rank, I believe, among the decisive battles of the war.

I am not speaking from hearsay. I was in France during the week preceding that battle, the most anxious and gloomy period, probably, of the entire war. What I am about to relate is based either on authoritative information gathered on the spot, or on my own observations. In telling it, nothing is farther from my thoughts than to wish to take away one tittle from the immortal glory which belongs to the Allied armies, nor from the undying gratitude which we owe to the nations who for four heartbreaking years, with superb heroism, fought the battle of civilization—our battle from the very beginning, no less than theirs and bore untold sacrifices with never faltering spirit.

JUST BEFORE THE TIDE TURNED

On the 27th of last May the Germans broke through the French position at the Chemin des Dames, a position which had been considered by the Allies as almost impregnable. They overthrew the French as they had overthrown the British two months earlier. Day by day they came nearer to Paris, until only thirty-nine miles separated them from their goal. A few days more at the same rate of advance, and Paris was within range of the German guns of terrific destructive power. Paris, the nerve centre of the French railroad system and the seat of many French war industries, not only, but the very heart of France, far more to the French people in its meaning and traditions than merely the capital of the country; Paris in imminent danger of ruthless bombardment like Rheims, in possible danger even of conquest by the brutal invader, drunk with lust and with victory! As one Frenchman expressed it to me: "We felt in our faces the very breath of the approaching beast."

And whilst the Hunnish hordes came nearer and nearer, and the very roar of the battle could be dimly and ominously heard from time to time in Paris, there were air raids over the city practically every night, and the shells from the long-range monster guns installed some sixty or seventy miles distant, fell on its houses, places and streets almost every day.

They were not afraid, these superb men and women of France. They do not know the meaning of fear in defence of their beloved soil and their sacred ideals. There was no outward manifestation even of excitement or apprehension. Calmly and resolutely they faced what destiny might bring. But there was deep gloom in their hearts and dire forebodings.

They had fought and dared and suffered and sacrificed for well nigh four years. They had buried a million of their sons, brothers and fathers. They were bleeding from a million wounds and more. They said:

"We will fight on to our last drop of blood, but alas! our physical strength is ebbing. The enemy is more numerous by far than we. Where can we look for aid? The British have just suffered grave defeat. The Italians have their own soil to defend after the disaster of last autumn. Our troops are in retreat. The Americans are not ready and they are untried as yet in the fierce ordeal of modern warfare. The Germans know well that in three months or six months the Americans will be ready and strong in numbers. That is why they are throwing every ounce of their formidable power against us *now*. The Hun is at the gate *now*. Immeasurable consequences are at stake now. It is a question of days, not of weeks or months. Where can we look for aid *now?*"

And out of their nooks and corners and hiding places crawled forth the slimy brood of the Bolshevik-Socialists, of the Boloists, Caillouxists and pacifists, and they hissed into the ears of the people, "Make peace! Victory has become impossible. Why go on shedding rivers of blood uselessly? The Germans will give you an honourable, even a generous peace. Save Paris! Make peace!"

165

The holy wrath of France crushed those serpents whenever their heads became visible. Clemenceau, the embodiment of the dauntless spirit of France, stood forth the very soul of patriotic ardour and indomitable courage. But the serpents were there, crawling hidden in the grass, ever hissing, "Make peace!"

And then, suddenly out of the gloom flashed the lightning of a new sword, sharp and mighty, a sword which had never been drawn except for freedom, a sword which had never known defeat—the sword of America!

THE TURNING OF THE TIDE

A division of Marines and other American troops were rushed to the front as a desperate measure to try and stop a gap where flesh and blood, even when animated by French heroism, seemed incapable of further resistance. They came in trucks, in cattle cars, by any conceivable kind of conveyance, crowded together like sardines. They had had little food, and less sleep, for days.

When they arrived, the situation had become such that the French command advised, indeed ordered, them to retire. But they and their brave general would not hear of it. They disembarked almost upon the field of battle and rushed forward, with little care for orthodox battle order, without awaiting the arrival of their artillery, which had been unable to keep up with their rapid passage to that front.

They stormed ahead, right through the midst of a retreating French division, yelling like wild Indians, ardent, young, irresistible in their fury of battle. Some of the Frenchmen called out a well-meant warning: "Don't go in this direction. There are the Boches with machine guns."

They shouted back: "That's where we want to go. That's where we have come three thousand miles to go."

And they did go, into the very teeth of the deadly machine guns. In defiance of all precedent they stormed, with rifle and bayonet in frontal attack, against massed machine guns.

They threw themselves upon the victory-flushed Huns to whom this unconventional kind of fierce onset came as a complete and disconcerting surprise. They fought like demons, with utterly reckless bravery. They paid the price, alas! in heavy losses, but for what they paid they took compensation in over-full measure.

They formed of themselves a spearhead at the point nearest Paris, against which the enemy's onslaught shattered itself and broke. They stopped the Hun, they beat him back, they broke the spell of his advance. They started victory on its march.

A new and unspent and mighty force had come into the fray. And the Hun knew it to his cost and the French knew it to their unbounded joy. The French turned. Side by side the Americans and the French stood, and on that part of the front the Germans never advanced another inch from that day. They held for awhile, and then set in the beginning of the great defeat.

I was in Paris when the news of the American achievement reached the population. They knew full well what it meant. The danger was still present, but the crisis was over. The Boche could not break through. He could and would be stopped and ultimately thrown back, out of France, out of Belgium, across the Rhine and beyond!

The aid for which the sorely beset people of France had been praying, had arrived. The Americans had come, young, strong, daring, eager to fight, capable of standing up against and stopping and beating back German shock troops specially selected and trained, and spurred on by the belief in their own irresistibility and the exhaustion of their opponents. The full wave of the hideous instruments of warfare which the devilish ingenuity of the Germans had invented, liquid fire, monstrous shells, various kinds of gases including the horrible mustard gas, had struck the Americans squarely and fully, and they had stood and fought on and won.

The French, so calm in their trials, so restrained in their own victories, gave full vent to their joy and enthusiasm at the splendid fighting and success of the Americans. The talk of them was everywhere in Paris. Hundreds of thousands of American soldiers already in France, thousands coming upon every steamer, millions more to come if needed—and they had shown the great stuff they were made of! All gloom vanished, overnight. The full magnificence of the French fighting morale shone out again—both behind the lines and at the front. "*Ils ne passeront pas!*" "*On les aura.*"

And the Bolshevik-Socialists, Soloists, weak-kneed pacifists, and that whole noisome tribe slunk back into their holes and corners and hiding places, and never emerged again.

And, as the people of Paris and the *poilus* at the front correctly interpreted the meaning of that battle in those early days of June, so did the supreme military genius of Marshal Foch. interpret it. He knew what the new great fighting force could do which had come under his orders, and he knew what he meant to do and could do with it. It is an eloquent fact that when six weeks later he struck his great master stroke which was to lead ultimately to the utter defeat and collapse of the enemy, American troops formed the larger portion of an attacking force which, being thrown against a particularly vital position, was meant to deal and did deal the most staggering blow to the enemy; and other American troops were allotted the place which from the paramount responsibility attaching to it, may be termed the place of honour, in the centre of the line, in immediate defence of the approaches to Paris.

They made good there—officers and men alike. They made good everywhere, from Cantigny to Sedan. They made good on land, on the seas and in the air; worthy comrades of the war-seasoned heroes of France and Great Britain, worthy defenders of American honour, ea- ger artisans of American glory. When, for the first time the American Army went into action as a separate unit under the direct command of its great chief, General Pershing, Marshal Foch allotted them ten days for the accomplishment of the task set for them, *i.e.*, the ejection of the German Army from the strongly fortified St. Mihiel salient, which the enemy had held for four years. They did it in thirty hours, and made a complete and perfect job of it.

I have had the privilege of seeing these splendid boys of ours, in all situations and circumstances, from their camps in America to the front in France—the boys and their equally splendid leaders. The sacred inspiration of what I have thus seen will stay with me to my last day.

I confess I find it hard to speak of them without a catch in my throat and moisture in my eyes. I see them before me now in the fair land of France—brave, strong, ardent; keen and quick-witted; kindly and clean and modest and wholly free from boasting; good-humoured and good-natured; willingly submissive to unaccustomed discipline; uncomplainingly enduring all manner of hardships and discomforts; utterly contemptuous of danger, daring to a fault, holding life cheap for the honour and glory of America. What true American can think of them or picture them without having his heart overflow with grateful and affectionate pride?

As I observed our army "over there," I felt that in them, in the mass of them, representing as they do all sections and callings of America, there had returned the ancient spirit of knighthood. I measure my words. I am not exaggerating. If I had to find one single word with which to characterize our boys, I should select the adjective "knight- ly."

A French officer who commanded a body of French troops, fighting fiercely and almost hopelessly in Belleau Wood near Château Thierry (since then officially designated by the French Government as the Wood of the Marine Brigade), told me that when they had arrived almost at the point of total exhaustion, suddenly the Americans appeared rushing to the rescue. One of the American officers hurried up to him, saluted and said in execrably pronounced French just six words: "*Vous—fatigués, vous—partir, notre job.*" "You tired, you get away, our job."

And right nobly did they do their job. Need I ask whether we shall do ours?

THE TIDE OF OUR GRATITUDE

The job now before us is to raise the needed funds to enable the organizations included in the United War Work Campaign to do theirs. No one who has not had occasion to see our army over there, can fully realise how much of comfort, of cheer and of home feeling these organizations are bringing to our boys. For, these boys with all their knightly virtues are very human. They are healthy young animals with strong appetites for food and for recreation. They will attack a dish of American ice-cream or a hot drink with a zest inferior only to that with which they attack a German machine-gun nest. They will crowd into an entertainment hut, a reading and writing or lecture room with an eagerness comparable to that with which they storm enemy positions. And they have an intense and touching longing for home.

The feeling of the long distance separating them from home is the one hardest to get accustomed and resigned to for those splendid fellows. The organisations of the United War Work, with the vast ramifications of their beneficent activities in all places where our army is fighting, training, constructing or resting are giving to the boys something akin to a home, something which brings the sweet and eagerly welcomed touch of American surroundings and atmosphere into the strange and unaccustomed world in which they are moving for the time being.

One must not think of those who are representing these organizations in their contact with the army, as bespectacled anaemic beings. They are, on the contrary, red-blooded men and women, with warm hearts and sympathetic understanding. The services and benefits of the great organisations they represent are open to any and every man wearing the United States uniform, irrespective of race or religion or antecedents. No questions are asked, and every one is made cordially welcome by the men and women who with devoted zeal, tirelessly, courageously and self-sacrificingly, often within reach of shot and shell, tend to the wants of our boys.

The spirit in which they administer their task is large and broad and of wide human sympathy and tolerance, as I can testify from personal observation. They realise fully that they are not dealing with saints or aspirants to sainthood, but with average youth and with soldiering youth at that. And they know what youth—clean, vigorous, normal American youth wants and appreciates in the way of material and spiritual things. They know the temptations besetting youth, but they also know that the normal American boy would far rather have clean enjoyment than tainted pleasures.

They are offering to all soldiers comfort, cheer, diversion, instruction, in short, the opportunity to gratify every legitimate aspiration, and if the records show that our army is the healthiest and cleanest that ever stood in the field, a large part of the credit for this enviable result belongs to the organizations included in the United War Work Campaign.

The extent of their work with its resultant inestimable benefit to our boys, is limited only by the greater or lesser liberality with which the country will respond to their appeal for funds—and, surely, no liberality can be too great towards those who fought without counting the cost in life and limb for our honour, glory and safety. And if, thank God, the fighting and maiming and killing have now come to an end, let us give in double measure as a peace-offering, as a thanksgiving, as a tribute to the memory of those who laid down their lives for America and for humanity.

Heaven forbid that we should permit an impression to go out to our soldiers that we took good care of them as long as we needed them to stand between us and the enemy, but that when the danger to us is past, we fail them. The debt of gratitude which we owe to them cannot be measured or discharged in money, but we can at least prove to them, as far as we can express it by giving, that we love them with proud and tender affection and that their well-being is a first charge upon our means.

America has broken many a record since we entered the war. There is one record yet to be broken before our boys come home. That is the record of the outpouring of a nation's gratitude to its defenders.

For some time past we have heard approaching in the skies, the beating of the wings of the Angel of Peace. Now he has descended upon our poor, bleeding, war-torn earth. He holds in his hands the great gifts of Freedom and Victory. We greet him with boundless gratitude and with reverent joy. The hideous idol of Prussian militarism lies shattered at the feet of the free nations, its archpriest dethroned and disgraced, cast out by his own distracted people and branded with the curse of the entire world.

To this blessed and glorious result, we may justly claim that America has contributed no mean part. We thank God for the day when, spurning the lure of ease and plenty and boundless prosperity, we chose for our own that road to the heights which leads through sacrifice and suffering and brought our mighty and unspent power to the rescue of the hard pressed champions of humanity. We then sought no advantage for ourselves and we seek none now. We have proved that America is not the "land of the almighty dollar," as too many believed and as especially our enemies fatuously believed to their undoing, but a land of high idealism, ardently zealous to do and dare and spend itself in a righteous cause.

We look back over these past fateful nineteen months and we examine our hearts and thoughts and deeds and we believe we may say justly and without self-complacency that the men and women of America have not been found unworthy under the great test to which they were put. Old and young, rich and poor, East and West, North and South—all but an insignificant few who are not spiritually Americans—have risen to the inspiration of our high cause and have joined in patriotic devotion and willing sacrifice.

A new and exalted spirit pervades the land. We have made a new pact of unity. We have come to understand and appreciate each other better. We respect each other more. We are justly proud of the qualities which all Americans have proved themselves to possess in common.

We draw strengthened faith and heightened inspiration from the glorious vindication of the irresistible potency of the American spirit which has made its own, transfused and merged into a homogeneous people, thinking and feeling alike in national essentials the men and women of many races who make up America.

We are now walking along the heights of great achievements and lofty aspirations. Let us shun the descent into the valleys we have left behind. Let us trust and strive that some at least of the things we have gained spiritually may never leave us.

America comes out of the war with her economic and moral potency and prestige vastly enhanced, with her outlook broadened, her field of activity expanded, her enterprise quickened, her imagination stirred, her every faculty stimulated.

The *vista* which opens before us of America's future is one of dazzling greatness, spiritually and materially. The realization of that vision cannot fail us if we but meet our problems in a spirit of true Americanism, of moderation and self restraint and of justice and good will to all, rejecting alike privilege and demagogy, banishing all class rule, be it of capital or of labour.

In that spirit let us grasp each other by the hand and thus resolved and united against enemies without or foes within, let us march on towards the high destiny that Providence has allotted to the country which in grateful pride and deep affection we call our own.

LEONAUR

ALSO FROM LEONAUR
AVAILABLE IN SOFTCOVER OR HARDCOVER WITH DUST JACKET

ESCAPE FROM THE FRENCH *by Edward Boys*—A Young Royal Navy Midshipman's Adventures During the Napoleonic War.

THE VOYAGE OF H.M.S. PANDORA *by Edward Edwards R. N. & George Hamilton, edited by Basil Thomson*—In Pursuit of the Mutineers of the Bounty in the South Seas—1790-1791.

MEDUSA *by J. B. Henry Savigny and Alexander Correard and Charlotte-Adélaïde Dard* —Narrative of a Voyage to Senegal in 1816 & The Sufferings of the Picard Family After the Shipwreck of the Medusa.

THE SEA WAR OF 1812 VOLUME 1 *by A. T. Mahan*—A History of the Maritime Conflict.

THE SEA WAR OF 1812 VOLUME 2 *by A. T. Mahan*—A History of the Maritime Conflict.

WETHERELL OF H. M. S. HUSSAR *by John Wetherell*—The Recollections of an Ordinary Seaman of the Royal Navy During the Napoleonic Wars.

THE NAVAL BRIGADE IN NATAL *by C. R. N. Burne*—With the Guns of H. M. S. Terrible & H. M. S. Tartar during the Boer War 1899-1900.

THE VOYAGE OF H. M. S. BOUNTY *by William Bligh*—The True Story of an 18th Century Voyage of Exploration and Mutiny.

SHIPWRECK! *by William Gilly*—The Royal Navy's Disasters at Sea 1793-1849.

KING'S CUTTERS AND SMUGGLERS: 1700-1855 *by E. Keble Chatterton*—A unique period of maritime history-from the beginning of the eighteenth to the middle of the nineteenth century when British seamen risked all to smuggle valuable goods from wool to tea and spirits from and to the Continent.

CONFEDERATE BLOCKADE RUNNER *by John Wilkinson*—The Personal Recollections of an Officer of the Confederate Navy.

NAVAL BATTLES OF THE NAPOLEONIC WARS *by W. H. Fitchett*—Cape St. Vincent, the Nile, Cadiz, Copenhagen, Trafalgar & Others.

PRISONERS OF THE RED DESERT *by R. S. Gwatkin-Williams*—The Adventures of the Crew of the Tara During the First World War.

U-BOAT WAR 1914-1918 *by James B. Connolly/Karl von Schenk*—Two Contrasting Accounts from Both Sides of the Conflict at Sea D uring the Great War.

www.ingramcontent.com/pod-product-compliance
Lightning Source LLC
Chambersburg PA
CBHW021106090426
42738CB00006B/520

"Tu libro es un compañero . . . como traer un amigo o amiga, incitándote a creer en un mañana más brillante y animando a otros a que intencionalmente configuren su vida para lograrlo. Uno fácilmente puede observar la profundidad y variedad de investigaciones que respaldan tu libro, haciéndolo, no solo alentador, sino rebosante con recursos. Sus esfuerzos tienen un potencial de largo alcance para bendecir a tantos más."

~ Maria Fischer,
Esposa, madre y proveedora de cuidado

"¡No podía bajar este libro! Escrito desde la perspectiva de su propia experiencia personal, Gale comparte cómo es que combatió su miedo dirigiendo su atención al conocimiento... ¡esto le infundió poder! ¡Comparte sus altibajos, buenos y malos días, pero claramente ilustra cómo siguió adelante con valentía y un nuevo amor por vivir una vida más saludable y dinámica! ¡Querrás leer este libro varias veces!"

~ Becky J. Hunter, administradora retirada,
Sandia National Laboratory

"En su relato sentido y compasivo sobre su experiencia, Gale lleva al lector a una nueva comprensión y paz al saber que una vida saludable se puede lograr después del cáncer. Un recuento sincero que es conmovedor en muchos niveles."

~ Clare O'Brien, vicepresidente asociada,
California Polytechnic State University, San Luis Obispo

"Gale es verdaderamente una de las personas más valientes que conozco y estoy bendecido para contar como amiga. Ella tomó una decisión consciente para hacer frente a la cabeza en una enfermedad y transformó su vida para vivir. A través de ella todo lo que ella ha mantenido una actitud positiva y un sentido del humor que ha sido una inspiración para mí. Transformación: Formando una vida excepcional al afrontar el cáncer me ha inspirado a buscar mis propios cambios de vida en el consumo de alimentos. Estoy tratando de vivir la vida de sonido más alimenticio posible".

~ Michelle McKinney, senior cost / analista financiero, USAF contratista